Agents of Opportunity: Sports Agents and Corruption in Collegiate Sports

Agents of Opportunity

Sports Agents and Corruption in Collegiate Sports

KENNETH L. SHROPSHIRE

UNIVERSITY OF PENNSYLVANIA PRESS   Philadelphia

Copyright © 1990 by the University of Pennsylvania Press
All rights reserved
Printed in the United States of America

Library of Congress Cataloging in Publication Data

Shropshire, Kenneth L.
    Agents of opportunity : sports agents and corruption in collegiate
sports / Kenneth L. Shropshire.
        p.   cm.
    Includes bibliographical references and index.
    ISBN 0-8122-8212-4 (cloth)
    ISBN 0-8122-1443-9 (paper)
    1. Sport agents—United States. 2. Sports—United States—
Corrupt practices. 3. College sports—United States. 4. Sports—
Law and legislation—United States. I. Title.
GV734.5.s57   1990
338.4'7796'0973—dc20   90-41858
                                                            CIP

First paperback printing 1992

Contents

Appendixes   111

Preface

Some of the recommendations I make in this book were first set forth in an article published in late 1989 in the *Cardozo Arts and Entertainment Law Journal* entitled "Athlete Agent Regulation: Proposed Legislative Revisions and the Need For Reforms Beyond Legislation." One of the proposals was for the NFL to allow underclassmen to be drafted. I was not alone in the recommendation, and certainly do not have the misbelief that any article was the catalyst, but a change did occur in early 1990 and juniors may now declare their eligibility for the professional draft.

Since the beginning of this decade, reforms in college sports seem to be moving at a pace not previously seen, in relation not just to the sports agent problem but to college sports in general. It is to be hoped that other reforms recommended in that article and here will be adopted, not because they were proposed here but because many others have been pushing for them for a while.

Part I of this book, "Background," describes what is currently taking place in the sports-agent industry. Chapter 1, "The Business," looks at the history of the sports agent industry and what it is that agents do. Chapter 2, "Unscrupulous, Unethical, Unqualified, and Criminal," takes a close look at the problems that exist in the business. The third chapter, "Knights of Columbus Rules: Existing Sports-Agent Regulations," sets forth the agent rules that have been put in place by private organizations. Chapter 4, "The Laws," presents an overview of the state laws as well as the legal actions that may be taken without the aid of these statutes. The final chapter in this section, "The Last Amateurs on Earth: Amateurism and Opportunity," looks at long-standing amateurism principles and how these may be responsible for many of the unethical activities of agents and student athletes.

Part II, "Changes," examines proposed reforms that have been presented by law or rule makers or that have developed anecdotally. Chapter 6, "Existing on Air? Pay, Employment, Loans, and Endorsements," looks at the possible effect increased compensation might have on the system. Chapter 7, "Let Them Turn Pro?" examines the influence the professional draft may have on the problem and the necessity of ensuring that the student athlete and agents are thoroughly educated on the rules of the industry. The eighth chapter, "Shake 'em Hard in the Sports Side," urges more rigorous enforcement of the existing laws and advocates reforms that would add competency requirements and consideration of the implementation of a national, uniform law. The final chapter reviews the reforms recommended and, as the title suggests, examines "The Future of the Business."

A point of style should be noted. The legally correct name for the individual that represents the athlete is "athlete agent," not "sports agent." More precisely, the individual is the agent for the athlete, not the sport. The term sports agent, however, has developed as probably the most commonly recognized and accepted label, so the terms "sports agent" or "agent" are used throughout.

Acknowledgments and Dedication

This book is the result of three years of formal research. For the past ten years I have worked in various aspects of sports representing athletes, agents, and other sports entities. At an earlier point in life I attended Stanford University with the aid of a football scholarship. That experience necessarily finds its way into these pages. Over the past three years, while formally researching this work, I have taught a course at The Wharton School of the University of Pennsylvania called Legal and Business Aspects of Sports. The comments of those hundreds of students wind their way into this work also. The statutory and other information in this edition is accurate through January 1, 1990.

A number of people were helpful in researching this book. An incomplete list includes: Craig Fenech, Charles Grantham, Dr. Michael Jackson, Edward V. King, Jr., Pam Lester, Roger Noll, Jeff Orleans, Reginald Wilkes, Dr. Wayne Wilson, Greg Smith and Reginald Turner. Invaluable research assistance was provided by Nicole King, Roslyn Levine, Henry Moniz, Michael Rivera, and Sankar Suryanarayan. A grant from the Fishman-Davidson Center for the study of the service sector made many aspects of this research possible.

A special thanks to Professors Lionel Sobel and Phil Closius for their comments on the manuscript. I hope that I have heeded Phil's initial advice to say something about the positive aspects of agents.

Thanks also to Art Evans, formerly of the University of Pennsylvania Press, who encouraged me to develop an idea for a book on the business of sports when I first arrived on campus, and to Phil Hoose, who gave me the final push to move ahead with the project. Thanks also to Deloris Jones for her management of the manuscript.

Finally, thanks to my mother and father who have always preached the importance of speaking up when something is wrong. This book is dedicated to both of them, Claudius and Jane Shropshire.

Introduction: License to Fish

> It didn't seem so wrong. It seemed as though I worked my
> whole life to get where I am, and at the same time, when it was
> presented to me, it was like this was the time I could start to get
> back some of the fruits of my labor.[1]
>
> *Paul Palmer, former star college football running back, regarding*
> *cash payments of over $5,000 he received from sports agent Norby*
> *Walters while a college senior*

Paul Palmer is not alone in receiving payments that violate National
Collegiate Athletic Association (NCAA) rules and now, apparently, federal law as well. Other student athletes have received such inducements
as interest-free loans, automobiles, clothes, concert tickets, airline
tickets, and insurance policies.[2] And this is not a recent phenomenon.
In 1979, after receiving $1,000 from agent Mike Trope, former Univer-
sity of Maryland football player Steve Atkins told *Sports Illustrated:*

> I knew I did something wrong. I didn't want the NCAA to do something to
> Maryland, but I just needed some money to pay some bills. I didn't want to sign
> with him, [Trope] but I just needed some money to pay some bills.[3]

The logic and attitude of these student athletes is not unique. Former college basketball star Eldridge Hudson summarized the attitude
of at least some athletes in a *Time* magazine cover story: "Once you get
out on the floor, it's a job, and you expect to get paid. If a kid is busting
his ass on the court, if somebody wants to buy a car, let him have it."[4]
    Why have these payments been made in violation of laws and rules;
why is it likely they continue today? Economists refer to such actions as
"opportunism." Oliver Williamson, in his work *Markets and Hierarchies,*
defines opportunism as "self-interest seeking with guile."[5] The self-
interest of sports agents is the right to receive approximately 3 to 5
percent of athlete contracts worth an average of $500,000. As a result
of this income opportunity, a wide range of techniques have been
developed to secure student athletes as clients. Payments to athletes
have become standard practice for some agents. Agent Jim Abernethy
told *USA Today* in 1987, "Everyone is being paid and signed. If anyone
says otherwise, they're really stupid, blind or they're lying."[6]

Cash payments may be supplemented by promises of drugs or prostitutes. Violence is not unknown. In 1987 a federal investigation of agents was begun after the alleged slashing and beating of an agent's associate by a rival agent; the investigation revealed that agents had threatened to "break the legs" of athletes who would not sign with them.[7] These criminal activities contribute to the corrupt image of college sports today. Gone are the "good ol' days" of raccoon coats, fight songs, and tailgate parties. Today college sports are often associated with scandal.

No one will dispute that violence and the use of drugs and prostitution is illegal. What has not been examined closely are payments agents make to student athletes to obtain them as clients. The heart of the problem is that uniquely American sacred cow—collegiate amateur sports. Collegiate sports is the last field in the world where athletes are supposed to receive absolutely no direct monetary compensation for their athletic prowess. All the athlete may receive, under NCAA rules, is room, board, tuition, and educational fees. An athlete who requires more is only in limited circumstances allowed to work to earn it.

This concept of amateurism becomes more problematic when one understands that the Greek amateurism that many perceive American collegiate sports to be founded on may have actually allowed amateur athletes to receive compensation. Classicist David C. Young maintains that amateur athletes in ancient Greece won prizes worth as much as the value of ten years' wages.[8] If this is the case, then why is so much energy exerted to ensure that collegiate athletes receive no compensation? And even if the Greeks were not compensated, why is it so important to retain this limitation today? This issue is a key element in the present agent-regulation problem.

What is being done to stop undesirable agent activities? First, federal prosecutors are taking action. In 1989, for example, sports agents Norby Walters and Lloyd Bloom were convicted and sentenced for racketeering, conspiracy, mail fraud, wire fraud, and extortion after a trial that showcased sports and entertainment figures like University of Michigan head football coach Bo Schembechler and singer Dionne Warwick. Second, nearly two dozen states have passed or are contemplating some sort of legislation to regulate agents (see Appendix II). Unfortunately, none of the laws passed or proposed thus far does anything to ensure agent competency. In fact, except for the higher price tag, registering to be a sports agent is as simple as obtaining a license to fish: complete a form, pay a fee, and you're a "licensed" sports agent.

What can be done to stop the corruption created by sports agents in collegiate athletics? The problem is not so complex. Improprieties occur because the opportunity exists to make money. The solution, in broadest terms, is simple too. Remove the opportunity to prosper by "cheating." Take away the opportunity with reforms that recognize the realities of college sports. That is what this book is about: the problems and the needed reforms.

I Background

Chapter 1

The Business

For many people, the life of a sports agent conjures up visions of a Hollywood lifestyle of fast cars and fancy clothes. Some sports agents refer to their profession as "the business," in much the way natives of New York or San Francisco refer to their towns as "the city." Successful agent Leigh Steinberg describes the stereotypical agent as "short and slick, he wears a gold chain around his neck and a diamond ring on his pinky finger; he's armed with a stream of fast talk and a package of promises to fatten his wallet at the expense of the athlete."[1] It is this flashy lifestyle that many agents point to as a prime reason for success in obtaining athlete clients. It is this image, too, that has been largely responsible for the popular negative view of sports agents.

Agent Norby Walters fits the stereotype. Walters signed an astounding number of first-round draft picks as clients during his first year in the business. Through his firm, General Talent International, Walters represented such black stars as Janet Jackson, Patti LaBelle, and Ben Vereen, and many pointed to the middle-aged Walters's success with African-American entertainment acts as the "magnet" for young African-American athletes, who reasoned, "if he can do it for them, he can put me in a Rolls Royce too." When Walters joined forces with Lloyd Bloom, a former Studio 54 discotheque bouncer, as the *New York Times* described it in 1989, "the plan seemed so simple. Mr. Walters, a prominent music booking agent, would join forces with Mr. Bloom, an enthusiastic, young former football player, and together the two men, both white, would woo black college athletes with the promise that they could do for the athletes what the booking agent had done for such black entertainers as Luther Vandross and Kool and the Gang."[2]

Robert Ruxin, in his book *An Athlete's Guide to Agents*, tells the story of another agent, who attempted to make student athletes believe he was black. According to two student athletes who encountered the agent, "I thought he was black, having spoken to him on the phone. . . . His actions were black. . . . Like, he walked with a slight limp. You know, how a lot of blacks walk, kind of cool. A strut."[3]

The truth is, the individuals who refer to themselves as sports agents and their level of success are as diverse as in any other industry. A further truth is that many agents are competent individuals who perform services within the scope of their abilities. According to Richard D. Schultz, the executive director of the National Collegiate Athletic Association, "A few unscrupulous people poison the whole barrel and everyone becomes guilty by association. The majority of people that represent athletes are top-notch people that do it with class and integrity."[4]

Who Needs an Agent?

Although sports agents often exude the heady glamor of life in the fast lane, in reality agents attract clients, to a large degree, by performing valuable services for athletes who are enmeshed in increasingly complex business activities on and off the playing field. Probably most important, they provide a level of parity in negotiations between athletes and the club or other entity they are contracting to perform for. The club management has had years to become expert negotiators, sometimes negotiating dozens of contracts per year. The athlete may have only one opportunity to negotiate a contract in an entire professional career. A sports agent, however, may have negotiated many sports contracts and is often a match for the negotiating experience of the management representative. Even an agent who has not negotiated dozens of contracts in sports probably has experience negotiating contracts in other business settings. Rarely does a student athlete possess similar talents.

Reginald Wilkes was a pre-medical student at Georgia Tech University. When he graduated from college he had no idea that he would be drafted and subsequently be named the National Football League's rookie of the year. Even with his serious academic background, Wilkes recalls, "I don't think I was mentally prepared to choose an agent or negotiate a contract." He adds that it would be difficult for *any* student fresh out of college to attempt to negotiate a contract without an agent.[5]

Scholars indicate that the athlete salary negotiation is the classic scenario where the use of an agent is appropriate. In their article "When Should We Use Agents?: Direct vs. Representative Negotiation," Jeffrey Z. Rubin and Frank E. A. Sander conclude that it is most appropriate to use an agent "when special expertise is required, when tactical flexibility is deemed important and—most importantly—when direct contact is likely to produce confrontation rather than collaboration."[6]

This is not to say that the use of an agent is mandatory. Until the agent became an accepted part of sports, athletes often negotiated their own contracts with management. They might or might not also have the documentation reviewed by an attorney or other knowledgeable third party. Notable "self-negotiators" have included Danny Ainge of the Boston Celtics, Alan Trammel of the Detroit Tigers, and Mike Singletary of the Chicago Bears.[7]

Nevertheless, there are reasons why self-negotiation may not be a good idea. In addition to the need for "expertise" and "tactical flexibility," the avoidance of confrontation is particularly applicable in the sports setting. The athlete must play for the team once the negotiation is complete. It is often necessary in these negotiations for the athlete's representative to sing the praises of the athlete. To counter this, in the paradigm of bargaining, the management representative must discuss the skills the player lacks, whether factual or not. When the goal is to make the athlete a member of the team, both literally and ideologically, it is easier for both parties to negotiate when the player doesn't actually have to brag, or invite management's criticism.

An intermediate measure between self-representation and employing an agent is to use a family member or close friend for contract negotiation. George Brett, Robin Yount, Jammal Wilkes, and Mike Shula are among the athletes who have taken that route.[8] Atlanta Hawks superstar, Dominique Wilkins, has had various contracts negotiated by his mother.

There are also those who say athletes should stay away from agents and have their contracts negotiated by lawyers. Edward Garvey, the former executive director of the National Football League (NFL) Players Association, is one of the strongest critics of use of people who call themselves agents. His greatest criticism of agents is the large fee that they charge. He recommends that athletes use attorneys who will charge for negotiation services at a standard hourly rate.

Still, the most common practice is for the athlete to be represented by an agent. Ruxin estimates that possibly one player on each major league team negotiates his or her own contract.[9] And, absent exceptional circumstances, it does seem to be in the athlete's best interest to use a competent agent. One of the conclusions of a 1977 congressional inquiry into professional sports was that "player agents are now generally accepted as permanent, highly visible, and at times positively beneficial element[s] in the sports labor relations process."[10] Senator John

Culver stated at the annual Sports Lawyers Association meeting in 1989 that, "when performed properly it's about as honorable a thing as you can do so these kids [student athletes] are not exploited."[11]

The Agent's Duties

The agent concept in sports is similar to that which has long existed in the motion picture, theatrical, television, and music sectors of the entertainment industry, although, of course, the names of the agencies and agents that receive thank-yous at the Oscars, Emmys, or Grammys—like the William Morris Agency or Michael Ovitz—are probably more familiar to the general public than are the names of even the biggest sports agents. The duties that agents undertake in the entertainment industry, however, are often more specific than those of the agent in sports. In the entertainment industry, it is common for a performer to have a group of advisers, including an agent, a personal manager, a business manager, and an attorney, in contrast with the athlete's search for *an* agent.[12] The combined fees for the entertainer's group of advisers have been estimated to equal 30–40 percent of the entertainer's gross income.[13] The "agent," in the entertainment industry, is loosely defined as the person who finds employment for the entertainer. This activity of finding employment is what distinguishes the agent from the entertainer's other advisers.

The agent in entertainment has been regulated by state laws for some time. Because of the nature of the entertainment industry the agent can be regulated by laws in New York and California alone, the states where the entertainment industry is centered. This situation contrasts with that of the sports industry, which is truly national. Indeed, the national nature of the sports agent industry is one of its major regulating problems. The entertainment industry does, however, have its unregulated side. The personal manager in entertainment wears many of the hats the sports agent does. According to the musical entertainer Kashif, personal managers often enter the business like sports agents, with no experience at all. Kashif quipped that it would not surprise him to hear a personal manager say, "Yesterday I was a garbage man, today I'm a manager." Fortunately, it is a generally recognized practice in the entertainment industry for the personal manager to hire professionals to handle the tasks of the combined team.[14]

The sports agent often provides services beyond the negotiation of the professional contract.[15] These additional services may include financial advice and money management, obtaining and negotiating endorsement contracts, counseling regarding the client's sport, post-player career counseling, and counseling regarding matters of everyday life. All these services and more are certainly required, in varying degrees, by today's professional athletes.[16] Once the player signs a contract, the agent may continue to have ongoing obligations, depending on the nature of the specific athlete/agent agreement. Some agents are finished with their duties once the player contract is negotiated and simply receive their fee. Others perform financial, endorsement, and counseling services.

A negative aspect of the business is what some agents refer to as "babysitting"—taking the 1:00 A.M. telephone call about the bad game the player had that night. As Atlanta based sport agent and attorney David Ware told a gathering of sports agents, "The good agents have to accept that as a part of the business. If you don't like being in the personal service business, it's [being a sports agent] not the business for you. You may not think the 1:00 A.M. phone call from a player is important, but obviously he does."[17]

Not all sports agents provide all the services an athlete may require. That too causes some confusion in the business. Most people today accept that professionals such as doctors or lawyers specialize in particular areas. You may go to a general practitioner, who will refer you to a surgeon to take care of the actual problem you are enduring. Likewise, your tax attorney may refer you to a trial lawyer. There are agents, however, who will attempt to provide services they are not qualified to perform for fear that they will lose their athlete clients by referring them to an expert, especially when the expert is (or is secretly anxious to become) a rival agent.

Full Service Firms

Some agents maintain that athletes not only want their contract negotiated but want to have the agent manage their income as well. Obviously, this is appropriate when the agent is qualified. In other cases, however, the agent may not provide adequate service. In fact, the agent may be violating state or federal laws if not properly licensed to perform this duty. To remedy this and similar problems, agents have recognized that special steps must be taken if they want to provide more than contract negotiation services. One solution is the full service sports management firm. The largest and most prominent are the Cleveland based International Management Group and the Washington, D.C. based ProServ, Inc. and Advantage International. These three firms provide, under one roof, individuals to negotiate contracts and to deal with financial issues, endorsements, and whatever else athletes might encounter during and even after their careers. Many prominent athletes such as basketball's Michael Jordan, golf's Arnold Palmer, and tennis's Jimmy Connors are clients of these firms.

The benefits of a full service agency are two-fold. First, the athlete is presumably able to receive the best service possible without having to shop around for various specialists. Second, the agent does not lose any part of the client's business. In fact, the athlete often pays an additional fee for any services beyond the initial contract negotiation. Where the cost of a contract negotiation may range anywhere from a low of 2 percent to a high of 10 percent of the total value of a contract, often an endorsement will cost the athlete as much as 25 percent of the value of the contract negotiated.

The marketing service a sports agent provides is not just a matter of pairing an athlete with some product that will pay the price. Although there is no special license required to be involved in product endorsements, an athlete can be harmed by an inexperienced representative. David Falk, a long-time agent with ProServ, observes that "sports marketing is a very specialized business. There is a very broad range of opportunities."[18] Falk notes that product choice is important and that the agent must be careful in determining "what kind of an athlete is appropriate to be utilized for a particular [product] campaign."

Not only is the product choice important, but so is the type of relationship the athlete has with the product. The athlete/product relationship may range from a one-day appearance at a local automobile dealership to what Falk calls the "autograph relationship" with a product. The autograph relationship is one where a product is named for a particular athlete, such as the Air Jordan athletic shoe manufactured by Nike and named after National Basketball Association (NBA) star Michael Jordan.

The agent must be particularly conscious of client overexposure. There is a view in the sports and entertainment industry that a client who is overexposed, or who appears in the public eye too frequently, will not be able to demand high endorsement dollars. The full service sports marketing firms pay particular attention to this issue.

Praise for full service firms is not universal. In fact, it is not difficult to interpret the practice of providing all services under one roof as a classic case of conflict of interest. Reginald Wilkes, Merrill Lynch account executive and former NFL star, makes the analogy of a union that hires a money management firm to run a pension fund. It is unlikely that the union would want the same firm also to evaluate the fund's performance, establish investment guidelines, and evaluate those guidelines as well. As Wilkes points out, such a set-up "invariably breeds an air of conflict of interest. The full-service agent firms are the exact same thing as far as I'm concerned."[19]

Edward V. King, Jr., a San Francisco based attorney who has successfully sued several agents for athletes, agrees with this as well. "It's like having all the foxes in the hen house. What you lose with a full service firm is a proper check-and-balance system."[20] Despite this warning, however, even King maintains that often the full service firm is the best place for the athlete to go.

Another alternative available to the athlete who wants agent services that go beyond contract negotiations is to pull together his or her own team of professionals. If the athlete is able to retain the approximate mix of professionals a natural check-and-balance system is established; each professional necessarily has some overlap with the others as well as the opportunity to review portions of their work in an unbiased manner. The athlete in this situation may, for example, hire an attorney to negotiate the player contract, an accountant to handle finances, an investment firm to handle investments, and one of the sports marketing firms to handle endorsements.

Competition for Clients

The nature of "the business" continues to evolve, and a major influence on its evolution is the competition for clients. Competition among agents is fierce. In fact, because of the competition, many individuals with outstanding business or education records are not able to sign a student athlete as a client.

One reason is the athlete's method of selecting an agent. As any athlete will attest, a prospective agent is not a difficult person to find. According to NFL defensive back Lou Brock, Jr., choosing a sports agent is "the perfect arena for a con man."[21] Consequently, the athlete's threshold question to the agent is often, "Who else do you represent?" This valid inquiry is sometimes the greatest barrier to entry for the prospective agent. One prospective agent described breaking into the business as being like the schoolyard basketball game "ice." In that game you are not allowed to begin to tally the baskets you score against your opponent until after you sink the first one. Sports agents face a similar dilemma: until you negotiate a contract for your first client you are frozen out while others with clients continue to score.

Dr. Michael Jackson, who is head of Temple University's Sports Management Program and directs Temple's agent screening program, does not give an agent without any experience much of a chance: "Surgeons have cadavers to experiment on. Our players are not cadavers. The agents have to have experience."[22] Agent Bucky Woy writes about the importance of that first client in his book *Sign 'Em Up Bucky: The Adventures of a Sports Agent:*

As far as Consulting Services' [Woy's firm] success in the sports agenting field is concerned, I owe everything to Mr. Easy [professional golfing great Julius Boros]. When he agreed to let me represent him in many business dealings, people took a new look at Bucky Woy and this consulting services outfit he was pushing. . . . He opened all the doors for me with the players who had been viewing me with suspicion during my first year in business.[23]

It is not surprising that Woy's entire book is dedicated to Boros. Similarly, sports agent attorney Bob Woolf closes his autobiographical work, *Behind Closed Doors,* by thanking his first client, baseball player Earl Wilson.[24]

Some agents, most notably Leigh Steinberg, boast that they do not solicit clients, that because of their reputations, athletes come to them. Baseball Hall-of-Famer Frank Robinson learned about his agent, Ed Keating, while appearing on the old television game show "Sports Challenge." Edward King says that, "typically, an athlete chooses Agent A over Agent B because Agent A has done more favors for the athlete or his family or has been friendlier."[25]

Phil Closius is an associate dean and professor at the University of Toledo College of Law. He also serves as an agent for some athletes in the National Football League and strives to provide his clients with quality services. Closius feels that, because of the standards in the industry regarding recruiting student-athlete clients, "there's no great benefit to providing people with good representation or by abiding by any of the rules that come out. . . .[26] The unfortunate circumstance is that if you go to a college senior and attempt to provide good sound advice and you don't offer some type of payment in most cases you look like an idiot." Closius sees this atmosphere as the main reason why the unscrupulous agent is likely to succeed while someone trying to follow the rules is likely to "be discouraged and drop out."

Because of the lucrative fees many agents receive,[27] the level of competition among sports agents to provide services and to obtain that first client has become extraordinary. As with any industry, as the field of competitors for a limited number of clients has increased so have the cutthroat methods of competition.

Payments to Athletes

Prior to the Walters-Bloom trial—and some say even now—there was a technique that had to be used to sign a student athlete as a client. Letters do not work, agents say, because students "don't write back and they receive dozens of pieces of mail." Even an eye-catching brochure featuring models, yachts, and sunny beaches in Miami and including an invitation to the athlete to come visit does not always attract the student athlete's attention. Mike Rozier, a winner of the Heisman Trophy, the award given annually to the best college football player in the United States, estimated that he received 1,200 letters while at the University of Nebraska, "most of which came from people I had never heard of, and who did not even know me, or want to know me. All they wanted was to line their pockets with the money that I soon would earn in professional football."[28]

It is the face-to-face meetings that agents maintain are most successful. Norby Walters gives a vivid description of what many agree occurs in face-to-face meetings between prospective agent and student athlete:

The kid knows everybody's breaking all the rules so he's primed and ready for a businessman to come along. He's talking turkey as soon as you sit down. "How much for my family? How much for me? How much interest? Do I have to pay it back?[29]

NFL linebacker Lawrence Taylor describes the tempering of the transaction in his autobiography. His first encounter with his soon to be agent Ivery Black came between his junior and senior years in college. Taylor explains that Black made it clear that the rules of the National Collegiate Athletic Association do not allow the giving of money; so his policy was to *lend* athletes money until they were drafted, after which they would repay the loan. This is a standard explanation of what appears to be a common practice.[30]

It is this transaction, and variations of it, that many see as the prime barrier to entry into the field by ethical professionals. According to Phil Closius, "The mentality on the part of the athlete is for 'right here and right now.' What can you do for me now?" Closius sees one of the agent's greatest contributions to the client as providing a perspective beyond the here and now. Any payment in the manner described by Walters and Taylor violates the rules of the NCAA.

The stories of what agents provide to athletes for their signing ranges from anecdote to fact. Leading the list is the report by *Sports Illustrated* that Walters and Bloom paid more than $800,000 in varying sums to approximately fifty athletes, five of those first-round picks in the 1987 NFL draft.[31] Similarly, agent Jim Abernethy claims that he spent more than $500,000 over a one-year period recruiting clients.[32] Other specific overzealous recruiting techniques include: the offer of one-third of an agent's management corporation to George Rogers;[33] the payment of a $2,500 promissory note to University of Alabama basketball star Derrick McKey;[34] the offer of $65,000 to former Louisiana State linebacker Michael Brooks;[35] the promise to Wayne Waddy, a running back at Texas Christian University, of $75 for each touchdown he scored;[36] the promise to a Memphis State University basketball player of $500 per month with a $200 Thanksgiving bonus and a $1,000 Christmas bonus;[37] the alleged payment to University of Iowa running back Ron Harmon, his girlfriend, and family members of $54,000[38] and an additional $1,500 paid to Harmon for revealing the phone number of a teammate to an agent.[39]

Harmon was also offered $2,000 to aid the agent in recruiting linebacker Larry Station.[40] In his autobiography, *The Boz*, NFL and former college star Brian Bosworth explains that other athletes are sometimes involved in the student-athlete recruiting process:

> You get hit on constantly by agents in college, or by friends of agents. Even pro players call and try to sign you with their guy. Howie Long of the Raiders called me to see if I wanted to hook up with his guy. I didn't even *know* Howie Long, much less his guy.[41]

Another client recruitment technique is the payment of a fee to the student athlete's coach or some other person with influence over the athlete. In 1988 *Newsday* exposed payments made by agent Lance Jay Luchnick to coaches. The investigation by *Newsday* revealed, among other payments, that Luchnick agreed to pay one coach, Ron Davis, a percentage of basketball star Cliff Livingston's contract if he could deliver him as a client. Livingston was "eager to help his old coach," and when he learned of this deal he signed with Luchnick.[42] Davis received over $14,000 for his role in bringing the two together.[43]

As if financial inducements were not enough, bribes are sometimes accompanied by threats. Chicago Bear free safety Maurice Douglas testified at the Walters-Bloom trial that Lloyd Bloom told him that "if I didn't return the money and the cars, he'd have somebody break my legs."[44] The reference to money and cars related to a $2,500 initial payment and other periodic payments made by Walters and Bloom; the pair also leased a car for him.[45] The *Chicago Tribune* reports that Walters and Bloom made "veiled references to their friends [in Las Vegas] as well."[46]

Many athletes and their parents, of course, evaluate the capabilities of potential agents as one would in the hiring of any professional. In the 1989 NFL draft first-rounders Troy Aikman and Deion Sanders both used extensive, formalized interview programs to select their agents.[47] Nevertheless, the interview techniques used by Aikman and Sanders appear to be the exception.

Agents' View of Their Business

One of the ironies of "the business" is that not only do outsiders look down on it but so do many of the agents themselves, if not always seriously, often sarcastically. One successful agent, Leigh Steinberg, for example, has called the sports agent business "the ultimate sleazoid profession of the '80s."[48] David Ware told a group of agents at a 1989 National Football League Players Association meeting, that he resented accusations that agents are a "little higher than snakes and a little lower than scorpions." Ware continued, "If you don't like the business, you should get out." In noting how much he enjoyed what he did, Ware argued that the agent has an "obligation to be a zealous advocate of his client."[49]

Ware's statements came in response to the constant grumbling of many agents regarding the difficulty in signing clients "honestly," that is, without making payments that violate NCAA rules. Ware has been successful. His representation of 1988 Heisman Trophy winner Barry Saunders in his negotiations with the NFL's Detroit Lions is just one of his achievements. In reality, however, most agents are not successful and they have not found the business to be financially rewarding.[50]

The position of sports agents entering the business illustrates why there is not a lot of success and numbers are a key factor. There are almost as many agents as there are athletes in the league; thus competition for clients is intense. Agent Bob Woolf estimates that there are 11,000 agents in the United States, well beyond the number of professional athletes in all the professional sports leagues combined.[51] Moreover, even if an agent does sign a client, there is no guarantee that the agent will make any money. If the athlete does not make the team after a contract has been negotiated, neither the athlete nor the agent gets paid; since the agent is generally paid a percentage of the athlete's earnings, the agent earns nothing if the athlete earns nothing. In exceptional circumstances, the agent may be paid on an hourly basis like most attorneys or accountants, and in such cases the agent may be compensated for the time put in. But such arrangements are rare.

Ironically, it is possible for an agent to exert the most effort for the athlete that is going to bring the lowest fee, the rookie free agent who is *not* drafted out of college. Often such a rookie will enlist a sports agent to help find a basketball or football team that is interested in giving him a tryout. The agent must then contact over two dozen teams in the appropriate leagues to try to find one or more that will give the player a tryout. If, after the tryout, the player does impress the team, then the agent can negotiate a contract for the player. But even then there is still the chance that the athlete will not make the team's final cut and the agent will not earn a fee for his or her efforts. Compare the work and the risk involved here to an early-round draft pick where there is no shopping for a team or a tryout and where the agent's responsibility is simply to negotiate a contract in the athlete's best interest. Although the contract negotiation itself may be difficult and time-consuming, the compensation to the sports agent will inevitably be higher than in the rookie free agent situation.

In the sport of baseball some agents exhibit the patience of Job while their clients serve time in the minor leagues, often for years. While this occurs the agent takes little or no fee while waiting for the call from the major league team to come. Most agents accept this toil with rookie free agents and minor leaguers as part of the price an agent must pay to become a success in the business. Among themselves, however, some complain about what a "pain" their athlete clients are. Ware notes that he for one "resent[s] guys who talk about the business and still take a fee for it."

The History of the Profession

The sports-agent profession is not a new one. What is new is the high finance and intense competition. Most attribute the genesis of the sports agent industry to the theatrical promoter, impresario, and show-man Charles C. "Cash and Carry" Pyle. Pyle was the agent for many athletes in the early part of this century, most notably the legendary football star Harold "Red" Grange,[52] the "Galloping Ghost." It was Pyle who negotiated a $3,000-per-game contract for Grange to play professional football with the Chicago Bears in 1925. In addition, he negotiated for Grange to receive over $300,000 in movie rights and endorsements,[53] including a Red Grange doll, a candy bar, and a cap. Pyle's other sports clients included tennis stars Suzanne Lenglen and Mary K. Brown.[54] Lenglen was the Wimbledon singles champion from 1919 to 1923. She signed with Pyle in 1926 for $50,000 to become the first professional tennis player.[55]

Another example of an early sports agent was cartoonist Christy Walsh. Walsh, according to *Sports Illustrated*, advised baseball Hall-of-Famer Babe Ruth to invest in annuities prior to the stock market crash of 1929.[56]

During the 1960s more growth was seen in the field and individuals from diverse backgrounds and professions became involved. For example, a great deal of press coverage was given to Hollywood movie producer J. William Hayes, the agent for actor Vince Edwards, television's Ben Casey, when Hayes orchestrated a $1 million "holdout" by Los Angeles Dodger baseball pitching superstars Sandy Koufax and Don Drysdale.[57] In a holdout, a technique used by sports agents to gain leverage in negotiations with a team, the athlete is, in effect, "held out" from playing with a team until the parties negotiate an agreement on the terms of the player contract. The Koufax-Drysdale holdout was for

$167,000 for each player for three years, an amount that was $42,000 more than the highest paid player of the day, Hall-of-Famer Willie Mays, earned. As part of their negotiating effort, Drysdale and Koufax signed with Paramount Pictures to act in a movie if their contract demands were not met.

Yet even in the mid-1960s the use of an agent by an athlete was a conspicuous event and received coverage in *Time*.[58] At the time, before settling the contract dispute, Dodger President Walter O'Malley told *Sports Illustrated*, "We can't give in to them. There are too many agents hanging around Hollywood looking for clients."[59] O'Malley's perception of the future was not far off.

The development of the sports agent as a recognized professional has by no means been smooth. One of the standard anecdotes of the industry is one told about the legendary coach of the Green Bay Packers, Vince Lombardi. It was time to negotiate center Jim Ringo's contract for the coming year. The player came into the office with a gentleman wearing a suit. Lombardi asked who the gentleman was and he was told by Ringo that he had come to help in the contract negotiation. The story has it that Lombardi excused himself, stepped into the next room, and made a phone call. When he stepped back in he informed Ringo that he was negotiating with the wrong team because he had just been traded to Philadelphia.

Lombardi was not alone in his view of agents. Another team executive, Don Klosterman, then of the Houston Oilers, told *Time*, "We spend $200,000 a year in evaluating talents and some uninformed agent is going to tell *us* what a player's worth? They're just parasites, in it for a fast buck."[60] Many believe that Klosterman's early blunt view was fairly accurate.

Obviously, acceptance of the sports agent by management has come a long way since the days of Lombardi, O'Malley, and Klosterman. It is now more common than not for a player to be represented by an agent. Schubert, Smith, and Trentadue, in their book *Sports Law*, conclude that the evolution of the sports-agent profession is not accidental, but simply a natural response to dramatic developments witnessed in the professional sports arena during this century.[61] The authors cite several events that have transpired during this time period to account for the prominent position agents currently possess in the sports industry.

One was the extensive use of reserve and option clauses in standard player contracts through the early 1970s. These clauses essentially bound athletes to teams in perpetuity without an opportunity to have their contracts affected by open market bidding. Beginning in 1972, however, the courts began to deliver rulings that invalidated the perpetual nature of these clauses. With this opening the athletes obtained increased bargaining power. The additional negotiating power created by these judicial rulings catapulted the players into a position of negotiating strength and hence higher salaries.

Second, competition from newly created leagues in football, hockey, and basketball presented the athletes with an appealing alternative to participation in the established leagues. Suddenly, the athletes had the ball in their court, so to speak. They were able to tell owners that they would command fair market compensation or they would take their services to the rival leagues. This demand led to higher salaries, which were simultaneously enlarged by the voracious appetite of the newly formed leagues to sign players of some fame. The signing of then Collegiate All-American Joe Namath by the upstart American Football League and the later signing of NFL veterans Paul Warfield, Larry Csonka, and Jim Kiick by the rival World Football League for astronomical salaries are examples. Roger Noll of Stanford University writes that interleague competition is an important cause of increases in player salaries. During the National Basketball Association–American Basketball Association wars from 1967 to 1972, the average salary increased from $20,000 to $90,000.[62] During the United States Football League (USFL) war, between 1982 and 1985, the average salary rose from $90,000 to $190,000.[63]

Third, the strength of the unions went from informal to the powerful position most hold today. Although the major sports unions have varying degrees of strength, they have all had an impact in increasing salaries, particularly the league minimum salaries. The unions have also been responsible for solidifying the role of agents, by leaving the role of salary negotiator to the agents and not retaining it for itself as unions traditionally do.

Fourth, tax planning became a necessity for athletes. The higher salaries made it necessary to get professional tax advice. Just as with any other highly compensated individual, the professional athlete is wise to obtain competent tax advice. The advice that the athlete requires is complicated by the fact that a playing career, in most sports, averages less than five years. With this in mind, the planner may have to take extra precautions to protect the athlete's earnings.

Fifth, additional sources of revenues began to emerge, both for the leagues and for individual players. Media interest in including sports as part of regular programming expanded very rapidly, pouring enormous amounts of revenues into the leagues. Using the muscle of their bargaining unit, the players' association, the athletes benefited handsomely from this revenue bonanza. Furthermore, this incremental media exposure helped widen the popularity of athletes, which resulted in a booming commercial endorsement business for the players.

These five elements and the increasing complexity of the clauses ·
required to protect athletes in player contracts caused the demand for
agents to increase. Two often referred to as the "modern fathers" of the
sports-agent industry for team sports are Boston based agent Bob
Woolf and New York based Martin Blackman.

Bob Woolf's beginnings in the business are chronicled in his 1976
book *Behind Closed Doors.*[64] A former criminal lawyer and college basketball player, Woolf entered the sports agent business in 1964. He
maintains that he was the first attorney to specialize in the area and that
as of 1976 he had negotiated more than 2,000 contracts. Woolf entered
the field by accident when professional baseball player Earl Wilson
came to his office for standard legal advice following an automobile
accident. According to Woolf, "When we talked we discovered we had a
lot of attitudes in common. One day we found ourselves discussing
methods by which an athlete could defer income and that, I guess, is
where the whole thing began."[65] Some of Woolf's most famous clients
include Carl Yastrzemski, Jim Plunkett, Julius Erving, and Derek San-
derson.

While Woolf is noted as a pioneer in the representation of athletes in
contract negotiations, Martin Blackman is best known for his pioneer-
ing negotiation of endorsement deals for athletes. His most famous
connection of athletes with products is the series of Miller Lite television commercials featuring retired professional athletes. Many point to
the early deals put together by Blackman as the foundation for the
growth in endorsement contracts today.

Probably the most successful agent of the 1970s was Mike Trope.
Trope writes about the success and tribulations of his career in his
autobiographical *Necessary Roughness,* published in 1987.[66] Trope entered the business in 1973 at the age of twenty while still a student at
the University of Southern California. Not only did Trope enter the
business at an unusually young age for any profession, but he did so
with an unusually prominent client: Johnny Rodgers, the 1972 Heisman Trophy Winner. This began an amazing string of signings by
Trope of six Heisman Trophy winners and other first round draft picks
in the sport of football. Trope negotiated a $1.6 million contract plus a
Rolls Royce for Rodgers from the Montreal Alouettes of the Canadian
Football League. His other clients included running backs Ricky Bell,
Tony Dorsett, and Earl Campbell.[67]

Perhaps it was Trope's success, other agents' jealousy, or simply the
truth that accounted for what were probably the first widely circulated
stories regarding improprieties in obtaining clients. When anyone
young in any business is successful it is natural to ask how it was done.
Whenever there is a young "whiz kid" in any industry he or she will

probably be subject to intense scrutiny. Trope was alleged, among other things, to have made payments to athletes to induce them to sign with him.

In his book Trope readily admits that "some things" occurred. He also makes it clear that he did not consider the rules of the NCAA to be the law of the land and so he had not, in his mind, done anything illegal. Trope alleges that his competitors started the stories about his illegal activities, and maintains that he was not alone in being involved in activities that violated NCAA regulations.

One successful competitor and one who remained in the business even after Trope retired is agent Leigh Steinberg. Steinberg, like Trope, started out at a relatively young age. While a law student at the Boalt Hall Law School at the University of California at Berkeley, Steinberg developed a relationship with an undergraduate student and star athlete, quarterback Steve Bartkowski. Steinberg was an adviser in Bartkowski's dormitory. Bartkowski became Steinberg's first major client, and at the age of twenty-five, Steinberg negotiated a then record $650,000 per year contract with the Atlanta Falcons of the NFL.

Steinberg continued to have great success and was noted not only for what were considered outstanding contracts for his clients but for being a master at public relations. His unique contracts often required that the athletes give a portion of their professional contract earnings to their colleges or high schools. But it was not just the terms of the contracts that brought him public notice, but also numerous positive quotes in the press as well as appearances on television shows such as "Lifestyles of the Rich and Famous." Through such self-promotion, Steinberg has developed a reputation as one of the few "honest" agents.[68]

While Steinberg and Trope became successful as individuals, two other sports agents developed firms that became and still are sports marketing powers: Mark McCormack's International Management Group in Cleveland and Donald Dell's Washington, D.C. based ProServ.[69] International Management Group (IMG) got its start in professional golf. McCormack's first client, in the early 1960s, was Arnold Palmer. Because of the firm's marketing and management successes with Palmer other golfers soon followed, including Jack Nicklaus and Gary Player. The firm eventually branched out into other sports and other areas of representation. In 1989 it represented such diverse clients as the Wimbledon Tennis Championships and the Vatican.

Donald Dell is an attorney and former captain of the U.S. Davis Cup tennis team. It is understandable, then, that ProServ got its start in tennis. Dell's first client was Arthur Ashe. Building on his success with Ashe, Dell began to represent other tennis players and, like IMG, eventually began to branch out into other team and individual sports.

By 1980 other agents had become prominent, some specializing in specific sports, others representing athletes in several sports. The agent ranks continued to swell, with even boxing promoter Don King being certified as an agent by the National Basketball Players Association.[70] Agents began to have their names closely associated with the athletes they represent. If one attends a sports agents' conference or an event where there are potential professional athletes, one can walk away with a wide array of business cards with firm names such as Sports Plus, The Sports Management Group, Superstars, Inc., and Sportstars. The owners of most of these types of firms are part-time agents and full-time stockbrokers, attorneys, accountants, insurance agents, dentists, or members of virtually any other profession. As we have seen, with the increase in the number of individuals in the industry the hostility between agents has also increased. Some agents jokingly refer to their ongoing battles as "agent wars."

Fact has blended with fiction to discredit the business with anecdotes, but not until the 1989 trial of agents Norby Walters and Lloyd Bloom were many of the anecdotal stories confirmed to the public at large. Nobody but the agent and the athlete client know how intense the competition has become or what type of recruiting tactics continue today. Many agents who have unsuccessfully tried to recruit clients without making payments or taking other steps in violation of NCAA rules cannot imagine someone making a living as a sports agent legitimately. Is this the reality or only sour grapes? The next chapter takes a close look at what did take place in the industry while competition was peaking and leading up to the conviction of agents Walters and Bloom.

Chapter 2

Unscrupulous, Unethical, Unqualified, and Criminal: Problems in the Sports-Agent Industry

The development of the sports agent industry and the increased competition brought about a variety of problems. Some were related to the quality of service provided by agents, but most, at least the most publicized, developed because of the stiff competition for clients. Public scrutiny of sports agents has reached an all-time high. The competition for clients, the front-page stories of the federal grand jury indictment, trial, and conviction of Walters and Bloom, and sad stories about student athletes who take several classes in subjects like billiards, all these factors have alerted the public to some of the industry's problems.

In the rush to quash the sports agent problems and regulate the industry an essential reassessment of the specific environment to be regulated is being overlooked. The view of most legislatures is similar to that of Florida's as expressed in the first section of its sports agent legislation:

The Legislature finds that dishonest or unscrupulous practices by agents who solicit representation of student athletes can cause significant harm to student athletes and the academic institutions for which they play. It is the intent of the Legislature to protect the interests of student athletes and academic institutions by regulating the activities of athlete agents which involve student athletes at colleges or universities in the state.[1]

In short, many agents are alleged to be unscrupulous, unethical, unqualified, criminal, or some combination of the four. At the end of the 1980s more than a dozen states had put into effect laws that attempted to regulate the activities of sports agents.[2]

Although appropriate legislation focusing on this industry should certainly prove beneficial, there are probably already state and federal laws in place that address any illegal activity in which the sports agent may be involved. Many of these are discussed in Chapter 4. It is necessary to examine the sports-agent activities that are not addressed, and that are considered undesirable by some, and why they continue to occur. This chapter examines many of the actual problems that do exist in the sports agent industry.

The payment of monies to student athletes by sports agents discussed in the previous chapter is the most publicized wrong done by sports agents, but there are many others that also occur frequently. These include athlete income mismanagement, the charging of excessive fees, sports-agent conflicts of interest, and aggressive client recruitment tactics. The following sections examine some of these improprieties.

Income Mismanagement

The stories associated with the mismanagement of athletes' income are no more dramatic than those involving doctors, lawyers, or other business people. When these incidents occur in sports, however, they receive much more publicity because of the notoriety of the parties involved.

At the heart of many athletes' financial headaches is the fact that agents are subject to few educational or professional requirements, the vaguest ethical standards, and minimum regulation. Ed Hookstratten, a Beverly Hills entertainment attorney who is also a sports agent, says, "I don't like to be lumped and called a sports agent. I was the Rams' general counsel for eight years. What I saw coming through the door representing the player was an embarrassment."[3] A former counsel to the NBA Players Association also criticizes deficiencies in the ranks of players' representatives: "A lot of people hold themselves out as being knowledgeable and competent. But the questions we get from individuals who purport to represent players are shocking. They don't understand player contracts, the collective bargaining agreement, or they simply don't understand the industry."[4]

One of the most widely reported cases of income mismanagement was that of retired Los Angeles Lakers basketball star Kareem Abdul-Jabbar. Abdul-Jabbar brought a suit against agent Tom Collins, which alleged that Collins mismanaged his client's basketball earnings by placing them in questionable investments including a rib restaurant in Texas, a hotel in Alabama, two hotels and a restaurant in California, an exercise rope, a sports club, a limousine service, a commodities brokerage, and a cattle feed business. There were also allegations of fraud.

As a result of this, in 1986 Abdul-Jabbar sued Collins and others for a reported $59 million.[5] The case was settled in early 1990; the settlement terms were not publicly disclosed.[6]

Another widely reported case of financial mismanagement involves Technical Equities Corporation, a growth-oriented holding company run by sports agent Harry Stern,[7] which declared bankruptcy in 1986. Technical Equities allowed individuals to invest in high-tech, manufacturing, and real estate deals. Many of the athletes had invested their life savings in the company. The firm's financial collapse involved not only seventy sports figures but nearly seven hundred others, including doctors and lawyers.[8]

In another incident, agent Jack Rodri was sued by two of his clients, NFL running back Eric Dickerson and former professional boxer Ken Norton. In separate suits both athletes alleged that Rodri mismanaged their earnings.[9] The Norton-Rodri suit was particularly shocking because Rodri had represented Norton throughout most of his professional boxing career as well as during his retirement.

In still another instance, NFL quarterback Jim Kelly sued his former agents for alleged gross negligence in the handling of his business affairs. That suit was for $130 million in damages, $28 million in punitive damages, and $200,000 in attorneys' fees.[10]

Actual criminal prosecution took place against agent Richard Sorkin.[11] While acting as a sports agent Sorkin gambled and lost in the stock market over $1 million in earnings of more than fifty hockey and basketball players. Investigations revealed that Sorkin bet as much as $100,000 per week on horses, baseball, and football.[12] The District Attorney in that case found that Sorkin lost $626,000 gambling and $271,000 in the stock market. Other missing funds could not be traced or otherwise accounted for.[13]

Similar to Sorkin's gambling was Lloyd Bloom's misuse of an athlete client's personal funds. In the Walters-Bloom trial Joel Levy, an accountant for both Lloyd Bloom and his client, then Kansas City Chief running back Paul Palmer, testified about the misuse. Levy maintained that Palmer gave Bloom $125,000 to start a credit restoration business. With these funds Bloom allegedly paid an $82,242 down payment on the lease of a $160,000 1987 Rolls Royce Corniche, commonly referred to as the most expensive vehicle in the world. He also used the funds to pay other personal expenses, including "credit-card debts, clothing and karate lessons."[14] Levy testified further that Bloom "had a sickness with money and trouble handling his own money."[15]

These abuse stories should not make us forget that there are legitimate financial success stories. *Sports Illustrated* reports that former major league outfielder Gary Maddox pays IMG $12,000 a year to manage his investments and has been very successful. Similarly, major league pitcher Orel Hershiser, a former business major, works with his agent to invest $1 million per year for an annual expected yield of $300,000 upon his retirement.[16] The number of success stories probably rivals the disasters, but it is the latter that receive extensive press coverage.

Excessive Fees

The charging of excessive fees is another problem. Players' unions have attempted to put ceilings on what agents can charge for contract negotiations. In 1988 the National Football League Players Association actually reduced the fee that a certified agent could charge a rookie client from 10 percent to 5 percent of the first-year playing contract. In reality the average fee for contract negotiations alone is around 3 percent of the value of the contract negotiated. It is rare that an athlete is unaware of the current rate.

The unions have taken steps to prevent another widespread impropriety exercised by agents: the receipt of the entire fee "up front" from the athlete's signing bonus or first few pay checks. As players have become more knowledgeable regarding the fees being charged by agents, this has been less of a problem, but the dangers are illustrated by the case of *Brown v. Woolf*.[17] In 1983 agent Bob Woolf negotiated a five-year $800,000 contract for a hockey player, Andrew Brown. Woolf received a fee of $40,000, or 5 percent of the projected $800,000 salary. The team, however, suffered financial difficulties, and Brown received only $185,000.[18] Consequently, the agent's percentage equaled more than 20 percent rather than the 5 percent contracted for.

Interestingly, the Major League Baseball Players Association has no limit on the fees an agent may charge. MLBPA Associate General Counsel Gene Orza maintains that the market will regulate itself. He argues that, because of the athletes' knowledge of the market, agents charging too much will soon be out of business.

Conflicts of Interest

Agents have also been under the microscope for engaging in practices where conflict of interest may be present. A conflict of interest occurs when a duty owed to one party is compromised by a separate interest or agreement with a third party. In the athlete/agent relationship an agent may have an agreement with another athlete on the same team, a team with which he is negotiating, or some other interest that conflicts with the duty owed to the athlete client.

According to *Sports Illustrated*'s Craig Neff, "[o]ther less obvious conflicts of interest abound when an agent has clients on different teams in the same sport, he's representing competitors—a conflict that would be unacceptable in any other field. The conflict is worse when the clients play the same position. For example, when Warren Moon left the Canadian Football League . . . [Leigh] Steinberg was put in the awkward position of shopping him to the New York Giants, who had another Steinberg client, Scott Brunner, playing quarterback."[19] Another thorny situation is when the agent represents various players on one team and the players are seeking remuneration from a limited fund, such as is the case in the National Basketball Association, where each team has a salary cap that limits the amount of money a team may allocate for player salaries. Agents often defend their conflicts by saying that their clients are fully aware of them. They assume that if the disclosure is made, the athlete can then decide whether or not the agent should be fired.

The conflict of interest issues in the athlete/agent relationship usually involve the non-disclosure of a financial interest of the agent's that conflicts with that of the athlete client. One case involved Philadelphia Eagles football player Reggie White and his former agent Patrick Forte. White alleged that while Forte was negotiating with the Eagles regarding White's player contract Forte was also negotiating a contract for himself to be an assistant to the president of that NFL franchise. In a suit filed in U.S. District Court in Philadelphia, White maintained that this constituted a conflict of interest and affected Forte's performance in his player-contract negotiation.[20]

A similar case was that of *Detroit Lions, Inc. v. Argovitz*.[21] That case pitted agent Jerry Argovitz against Detroit Lions running back Billy Sims. Argovitz was negotiating for Sims with both the NFL's Detroit Lions and the then competing United States Football League's Houston Gamblers. Throughout his negotiations with the Lions and the Gamblers Sims was unaware that Argovitz had an ownership interest in the USFL franchise. Although Argovitz had told Sims that he had applied for the Houston franchise and although Sims had attended the press conference at which Argovitz had announced that his USFL application was approved, the court found that Argovitz could not have expected Sims to understand the extent to which his agent's interest and position as president of the team undermined his efforts as an unbiased third party negotiator. When Argovitz's application for the Gamblers' franchise was approved, Argovitz reduced his offer on behalf of Sims to the Lions and dropped prior demands for so-called skills guarantees that had the potential to provide Sims with even greater income. While these negotiations continued, Argovitz decided to seek an offer from the Gamblers and provided one of his partners with information regarding the offer Sims had received from the Lions. Meanwhile, based on the information about the progress in negotiations that came from Argovitz, Sims believed that the Lions were not interested and did not urge Argovitz to seek a final offer from them. The court concluded that Argovitz knew the reasons behind Sims's decision not to ask Argovitz to contact the Lions to request any matching offer and that Argovitz breached his duty to contact the Lions and receive and present their final offer alongside that of the Gamblers to Sims.

The court concluded that to deny rescission of Sims's contract with the Gamblers would be unconscionable in view of Argovitz's egregious and pronounced breach of his fiduciary duty to Sims during negotiations on behalf of Sims with the Lions. As the court pointed out, "Argovitz's conflict of interest and self-dealing put him in the position where he would not even use the wedge he now had to negotiate with the Lions, a wedge that is the dream of every agent."[22] This "wedge" was the offer from a franchise in a rival league. Argovitz knew that if he called the Lions, the Lions would offer Sims a contract and Sims would not be available to the Gamblers, which Argovitz owned. Moreover, Argovitz had Sims sign a waiver without telling Sims to obtain advice independently, arranged a $500,000 loan from the Gamblers to Sims at 1 percent above prime, out of which he knew his $100,000 fee would be paid, and did not demand benefits for Sims, a proven NFL talent, comparable to those which Jim Kelly, another player, obtained from the Gamblers.[23]

Probably the longest running conflict of interest allegations involve not team sports but professional tennis. In ongoing court proceedings IMG and ProServ have been challenged regarding the propriety of representing tennis players and managing the major tennis competitions as well.[24] The two sports marketing firms also represent several major tournaments as well as sponsors of the events such as Volvo and Ebel. This scenario is the classic configuration of a monopoly: a few entities controlling the entire marketplace.[25]

Another agent conflict occurs when leaders of players' unions represent individual union members in their contract negotiations with their respective teams. The argument against this asserts that the union leader's primary responsibility is to safeguard the rights of all union members and that there may be circumstances where an act may be advantageous to the union leader's client but not to the union as a whole or where an act could be advantageous to the union but not to the individual athlete.

The late Larry Fleisher, former head of the National Basketball

Players Association, represented individual athletes while he was the union leader. Similarly, former National Hockey League Players Association chief Alan Eagleson represented individual athletes in that league. Eagleson's conflicts in representation and other areas became so extreme that the members of the union initiated an independent investigation of his interests in 1989.[26]

Agent David Falk notes that it is not the existence of a conflict alone that is a problem. "The question is whether you have a debilitating conflict." Falk and others maintain that because of the limited number of agents with actual expertise in sports business issues most successful agents are bound to have conflicts: "Invariably you're going to have conflicts even if you only have two clients." Falk makes a valid point. If an endorsement deal is offered to an agent to give to either of his two clients, only one can be given the deal and necessarily the other is shortchanged.

Who Is Being Harmed?

In general, potential clients may be divided into two groups. The first is comprised of individuals leaving the National Collegiate Athletic Association as amateurs and turning pro. Up to this time the student athlete has been required to live under the strict regulations imposed by the NCAA. These constraints are the primary cause of the "opportunity" presented to the sports agent to act in a manner many consider to be unethical. And it is at this juncture that inducement payments take place. The greatest scrutiny is placed upon the relationship between the student athlete and the sports agent. Acts by the sports agent that affect the student athlete have most consistently prompted the cries for the regulation of sports agents.

The second group is comprised of athletes who are already professional. Generally, the professional athlete is older and requires an agent who will provide services beyond the initial contract negotiation that is the primary interaction between the sports agent and the student athlete. The public has shown little concern about whatever payments agents may make to *these* professionals to induce them to become clients. Most criticisms of agents at the professional level involve income mismanagement.

The prevalence of unscrupulous and unqualified agents persists because opportunity exists. The opportunities that exist are not necessarily ones that can be restricted by legislation. For example, legislation banning cash payments or loans from sports agents to student athletes does not remove the opportunity for someone to give student athletes money. In support of this, sports law specialist John Weistart points out,

The incentives are sufficiently strong and the chance for indictments sufficiently remote that it will probably continue if we put in jail every athlete and agent who engages in an improper payment, I'm not sure there would be enough jails and prisons in the country to accommodate them.[27]

Most student athletes require more money than they can get through their scholarships. Thus, the solution may not be a law restricting payments, but a reexamination of the financial requirements of student athletes and a reassessment of what money they may receive while participating in college sports.[28] The NCAA has taken a first step in this regard by studying the status of the student athlete. The report found that, on average, college football and basketball players have about $82.00 per month for expenses beyond room, food, tuition, fees, and course-related books. This compares with $114.00 for students involved in other extra-curricular activities. Although this amount is not dramatic, a disparity does exist. A student athlete who desires to close this gap is at a further disadvantage. As we will see, it is not always possible for the student athlete to accept part-time employment since holding a job may violate NCAA rules.[29]

The financial disparity between student athletes and their peers and the effect it may have on the student athlete is being ignored by individual state legislatures. Many state legislatures support what many consider to be outdated concepts of amateurism and the college athlete. Many state legislatures such as Mississippi, Tennessee, and Texas are incorporating NCAA definitions of what an amateur athlete is. At the core of the problem is the NCAA view of amateurism and its corresponding rules, which bar athletes from receiving or even earning anything beyond tuition, room, board, and educational fees.

It is not a novel proposition that often, perhaps too often, we look to legislatures for resolution when some segment of society is malfunctioning. At times, the result of such legislative intervention is too much added bureaucracy and too little actual problem solving. This appears to be the situation that is developing regarding sports agents.

In its present form, neither sports-agent-specific state nor federal legislation is the absolute solution to the growing problem. In fact, the most publicized prosecution to date, that of Norby Walters and Lloyd Bloom, cited existing federal laws aimed at illegal behavior in general, not specifically at the sports agent. Even the earlier, highly publicized prosecution of agent Richard Sorkin involved general New York State criminal laws. Thus the enforcement of existing laws may serve as a major source of alleviation. Still, specific sports agent legislation can be effective as well if it is designed to deal with the problems in the industry rather than simply to support outdated concepts of amateurism. One commentator notes that a possible explanation for increased legislative activity regarding sports agents is that the laws serve to "get people off the politicians' back."[30]

Sports agents take what may be considered unethical steps to obtain student athletes as clients largely because the opportunity exists to do so.[31] And the opportunity exists because of the long-held view in the United States of what a student athlete and amateurism are.[32] State legislatures should move with caution in adopting these standards.

As agent Mike Sullivan puts it, "You're never going to eliminate the problems, because desperate people [sports agents] are always going to do what they can to compete."[33]

Chapter 3

Knights of Columbus Rules: Existing Sports-Agent Regulations

With the growth of problems in the sports agent industry many concerned parties have sought to arrest the wrongs that are occurring. Most state legislatures truly had the best interest of the athlete in mind when they developed rules to regulate the agent/athlete relationship. Some, as in the case with any legislation, saw introducing a law as a way to "score points" with important constituencies. Lloyd Shefsky, the former president of the Sports Lawyers Association, in a comment on the status of regulation under Canadian and U.S. laws, reminds us that as the laws presently stand sports agents may legally practice their profession from prison.

The key entities involved in the regulation of sports agents are the NCAA, the NCAA member institutions, professional sports leagues, teams, players' unions, state and federal law enforcement and legislative entities, and, of course, the professional athletes, student athletes, and sports agents themselves. This chapter examines the rules of private entities, and Chapter 4 looks at the public regulations promulgated by state and federal laws.

Of all these entities the group with the least incentive to enter the regulatory field is the professional leagues. Sports agent problems have little direct impact on the leagues in general. It is the colleges, with their allegiance with and commitment to the NCAA, who have the greatest incentive. The discussion below sets forth a description of the various private parties and the relative effectiveness of any legal power they possess to control the activities of sports agents.

In simplest terms, the NCAA, through its member institutions, trains and supplies athletes for professional football, basketball, and to a lesser degree baseball. The intermediary in this transition from college to professional sports is the sports agent. If a student athlete is not drafted he may choose to retain a sports agent to aid him in determining an appropriate team to approach for a "free agent" tryout.

The teams in professional sports are members of leagues. The relationships between the teams and the league are set forth in their respective constitutions and bylaws.

The final major private party involved in agent regulation is the players' association or union. The players' associations are basically the trade unions for the athletes in the professional sports.

National Collegiate Athlete Association

The NCAA is the oldest and most powerful governing body in college sports. The NCAA developed as the result of a meeting in 1905 of thirteen colleges that met to discuss safety reforms in college sports. The meeting was convened at the urging of President Theodore Roosevelt following deaths and other serious injuries that resulted from the violent brand of football being played at the time.[1] In 1989 the association had over 1,000 members, 800 of which were colleges and universities commonly referred to as member institutions.

Although the NCAA sometimes appears to be a monolith of sorts, it is important to emphasize that its actions are the joint decisions of the 1,000 members. Richard Schultz, the executive director, defines the organization's basic premise as "institutional control of intercollegiate athletics."[2] Schultz describes his position as "so powerful I can't make a rule and can't change a rule," emphasizing that as an individual he does not feel that he wields a great amount of power to make changes. The constitution and bylaws of the association set forth the rules governing eligibility of student athletes. These documents, as revised, are published annually in the *NCAA Manual*. The professional staff of the NCAA is there to assist members in the interpretation of these rules. Within the rules are the specific guidelines setting forth the type of relationship a student athlete may have with a sports agent and still maintain collegiate eligibility. NCAA Constitution section 12.3.1 states:

An individual shall be ineligible for participation in an intercollegiate sport if he or she ever has agreed (orally or in writing) to be represented by an agent for the purpose of marketing his or her athletics ability or reputation in that sport. Further, an agency contract not specifically limited in writing to a sport or particular sports shall be deemed applicable to all sports and the individual shall be ineligible to participate in any sport.

Despite the huge domain the NCAA is chartered to regulate, the association does not have any legal strength to fall back upon. In fact, the authority that the NCAA wields is primarily economic. The NCAA has the power to impose sanctions against a member institution for violating association rules. The sanctions take various forms, but they can include barring a member institution from television appearances and post-season play, which generally guarantee considerable profits for a college sports program or university budget. This authority provides the NCAA with the strength to govern, since schools hesitate to jeopardize such revenue-laden opportunities as participation in the NCAA basketball national championship tournament, which can bring a school millions of dollars.

One of the most stunning examples of the NCAA's power is the so-called "death penalty." When the NCAA asserts this sanction a member institution is barred not only from championship competition but potentially from playing altogether for two years. The first school to receive this sanction, due to extensive recruiting and other violations, was Southern Methodist University. In 1987, SMU received a one year version of the penalty for paying thirteen players a total of $61,000 from a slush fund. The payments were approved by the SMU athletic department. When the sanction was imposed, the athletes were allowed to transfer to other schools. The projection by experts at the time was that it would take at least five to six years to rebuild SMU's program following the death penalty.[3]

Lesser penalties of probation can be devastating as well. In 1989 the University of Kentucky's basketball program was placed on a three-year probation for recruiting and other violations. The *Sports Industry News* estimated that the school would lose $1.8 million over the three years. Kentucky's initial losses due to the NCAA sanction were $350,000 from the 1988 NCAA basketball tournament, $250,000 from their share of their conference's television syndication package, and $1,100,000 from their conference tournament.[4]

Contrasting with this wide financial power over member institutions is the limited power the NCAA has over sports agents. According to Schultz, sports agent improprieties are "really one of the knottiest problems we have because there is not a lot we can do about it. All we can do is penalize the institution or the athlete."[5] It is probably this weakness that provides one of the greatest opportunities for sports agent improprieties. As of 1989, all that the NCAA had been able to put in force was a voluntary sports agent registration system, described in a memorandum that the NCAA distributes with its registration forms.[6] Under this system sports agents were required to complete a form, return it to the NCAA, and agree that they would not contact a student athlete or coach without first contacting the athletic director at that member institution. The NCAA memorandum explains that the

NCAA makes available, to the student athlete and others, a list of the individuals that have registered under this program.

This registration system was *voluntary* and the NCAA recognized in its memorandum that it operates without the force of law behind it. Former sports agent Mike Trope put the general weakness of the NCAA most succinctly in his book *Necessary Roughness* when he wrote, "The NCAA rules are not the laws of the United States. They're simply a bunch of hypocritical and unworkable rules set up by the NCAA. I would no sooner abide by the rules and regulations of the NCAA than I would the Ku Klux Klan."[7] Similarly, athlete agent Norby Walters told a *Sports Illustrated* reporter, in reference to an NCAA rule forbidding student athletes to contract with sports agents before their classes graduate, "I'll sign anyone I want. The NCAA can't enforce [its rules]. I'll sign a sophomore if I want."[8] Much like Trope, he told *USA Today* that breaking NCAA rules is "like saying we bent the Knights of Columbus rules."[9]

In 1989 some NCAA members began to acknowledge that it was possible that the voluntary agent registration system might have been doing more harm than good. Agents who registered could then tell prospective student-athlete clients that they had a registration "validation" from the NCAA. In fact, all the registration validates is that the agent has taken the time to complete a form. NCAA Executive Director Richard Schultz himself referred to the system as "meaningless,"[10] and at the end of 1989 it was abolished.

Players' Associations

Players' associations also have an interest in regulating athlete/agent relationships. These unions operate under the guidelines of the National Labors Relations Act (NLRA).[11] They were initiated by the National Football League Players Association (NFLPA), whose lead was followed by the National Basketball Players Association (NBPA) and later by major league baseball's counterpart, the Major League Baseball Players Association (MLBPA). These unions require sports agents to register with them and to receive "certification" before representing members of their unions.[12] The NFLPA and NBPA process basically requires the completion of a form, attendance at a seminar, and the payment of a fee. The MLBPA does not allow a sports agent to register until he or she actually agrees to represent a client.[13] The sanction for non-compliance with the rules set forth by the unions is "decertification." Although this is a relatively new rule for players' unions, it appears that it may have some effect on the sports-agent industry. In 1988 the NBPA decertified one agent for improprieties and declared all basketball-related contracts negotiated by that agent void.[14] Similarly, the *Philadelphia Inquirer* reported that the NFLPA had certified a sports agent for alleged problems in "the handling of clients' funds."[15] Robert Ruxin also writes that the NFLPA refused to renew an agent's certification because he forged a power of attorney.[16] The NFLPA maintains that confidential hearings have been held regarding other agents as well.

The unions seized this power to certify as a compromise between the existing functions of sports unions and traditional union functions. In most industries, unions negotiate terms and conditions of employment as well as all member salaries. In the major professional sports leagues, the unions negotiate minimum salaries and all other standard contract terms. The sports agent negotiates for all salary above that minimum.

In 1983 the NFLPA asserted the authority that they maintain inherently exists in unions and mandated that those agents wishing to represent union members be certified by the union. The unions actually assert their authority to regulate agents by requiring their members to deal only with certified agents and requiring teams to negotiate only with certified agents.[17] For example, the MLBPA asserts its authority in the MLBPA regulations by citing the NLRA, emphasizing that it is "the exclusive representative for all the employees in such unit,"[18] and then cites its collective bargaining agreement with management, noting that players may negotiate contracts with teams "in accordance with the provisions set forth in this Agreement."[19] The certification requirement is solidified by a further requirement in the Major League Baseball Collective Bargaining Agreement (effective June 17, 1988) that a player may use an agent for negotiations "provided such agent has been certified to the Clubs by the Association [MLBPA] as authorized to act as a Player's Agent for such purposes."[20] Gene Orza of the MLBPA noted that in the first nine months only one team had negotiated with an agent that was not certified, and in that case the team official admitted that negotiating with the uncertified agent had been unintentional.[21]

Initially, a key flaw in the NFLPA system was that the union did not represent student athletes until they signed a professional contract.[22] Thus the relationship where the greatest problems were occurring, with the recent graduate, was not covered by the regulation. The NFLPA now asserts its authority over the interests of the rookie athlete as well.[23] This contrasts with the NBPA, where student athletes drafted by the league have been considered to be members of the union since the creation of its agent regulatory rules.[24]

Interestingly, the MLBPA's primary goal is education as opposed to punishing the shady agents. According to Gene Orza, assistant general counsel of the association, "we do not think that agents are bad. We believe players should have more information at their disposal when they go about choosing an agent."[25] The MLBPA system strives to make this information available.

Players' association certification obviously carries more force than the NCAA program did. The strength in the union certification programs lies in the ability of the players' associations to decertify or even to deny initial certification of an agent. The NCAA had no similar power to decertify. However, union regulations run the same risk as the NCAA system of "validating" an agent without a thorough evaluation. Some agents do not want to register. Orza notes that one attorney maintained, "I am not an agent, I am an attorney," and has been fighting the registration requirement on that basis.

At the end of 1989 the NFLPA certification system was on the verge of extinction. Due to labor disputes with management the NFLPA had begun to move forward with plans to decertify the union. (The union ultimately decertified itself.) The decertification of the union meant that the agent certification program in that league had been eliminated and a voluntary program had been installed. Without this program, a lot of ground that had been gained in the regulation of football agents may be lost.

Association of Representatives of Professional Athletes

The agents themselves have a set of self-regulating rules established through their Association of Representatives of Professional Athletes (ARPA).[26] This organization, composed of approximately 120 members, is a self-regulatory agency formed by agents to reform their industry. Membership in the organization is voluntary, as is compliance with the organization's rules. Although ARPA has its own code of ethics, there is no entity that mandates their enforcement. The code of ethics is set forth in Appendix I. It has received high praise from some circles; however, ARPA has virtually no power to implement its enforcement.

American Bar Association

Many attorneys serve as sports agents. The American Bar Association (ABA) does not have regulations specifically aimed at sports agents. However, the Model Code of Professional Responsibility does apply to attorneys acting as sports agents,[27] and many states have adopted some form of these ABA regulations.[28] But no matter how effective any of these regulations may be they apply only to individuals licensed to practice law, and all sports agents are not lawyers. As we noted in Chapter 1, agents come from all walks of life, and the earliest agents appearing in the popular press were not attorneys: Pyle was a promoter, Walsh was a cartoonist, and Hayes was a Hollywood producer.

Besides the general problems of ethics facing all agents, attorneys also are subject to provisions in their Code of Professional Responsibility against solicitation of clients. Many agents, attorneys and non-attorneys alike, maintain that they do not solicit. The nature of the sports-agent business, of course, virtually mandates that the agent contact the potential client, rather than the other way around, which is the traditional route for the attorney, and non-lawyers are allowed to solicit student-athlete clients. Although recent U.S. Supreme Court rulings seem to indicate that the stiff rules against soliciting by lawyers have been softened, there are obvious problems if they remain in place,[29] since they place lawyers at a disadvantage in regard to those parties who are not restrained by the same sort of ethical guidelines. This means that the individual who may have the best training to represent athletes has the greatest barrier to entering the field.

Nevertheless, it appears that the rule against solicitation has not been a great hindrance to attorney agents. Many, to avoid any conflict with the rules, have established separate divisions for the athlete-representation portion of their business. For example, an attorney may carry one business card that reads "John Smith, Attorney at Law" and another for his sports agent business that reads "John Smith & Associates," thus theoretically circumventing any problems of solicitation as an attorney.

This chapter has tried to provide an overview of private sector attempts to regulate agent conduct. An equally important, and more widely discussed, area is government regulation. The next chapter examines the state and federal laws affecting the sports agent.

Chapter 4
The Laws

While private organizations have tried to regulate the sports agent industry, individual states have begun attempting to arrest the athlete/agent problems as well. Federal efforts have lagged behind. This chapter examines regulations governing sports agents as well as some of the legal actions that can be brought under non-sports-agent-specific laws by individuals harmed by some sports-agent activity.

State Regulation

There are two tiers of state regulation over sports agents. The first level is standard civil and criminal laws that may cover any improprieties in negotiating and drafting of contracts by sports agents or anyone else. The second is the new breed of sports-agent-specific statutes. In 1989 the states incorporating sports-agent statutes were Alabama, Arkansas, California, Florida, Georgia, Indiana, Iowa, Kentucky, Louisiana, Maryland, Michigan, Minnesota, Mississippi, Nevada, North Carolina, Ohio, Oklahoma, Pennsylvania, Tennessee, and Texas.[1] Other states including Nebraska and New York had legislation pending.

States with sports-agent-specific statutes are asserting their authority to protect the public interest by regulating sports-agent activities.[2] State laws generally fall into two broad categories: those that actually require agents to register in some manner and those that do not. The key provisions of selected state regulations are summarized in Appendix II. The objective underlying some of these statutes is to establish a certification procedure for individuals entering the field of athlete representation or continuing in it.[3] Many of the states with athlete/agent-specific statutes require the registered sports agent to post a surety bond.[4] Georgia is the only state in this group that limits the recovery of damages to the amount of the surety bond.[5]

All the agent-specific statutes protect student athletes currently enrolled in college. A few extend their coverage to include those athletes
who, although not enrolled in an institution of higher education, remain eligible to participate in intercollegiate sports,[6] while other statutes provide universal protection to all resident athletes engaged in
any team sport.[7] Georgia and Texas extend the scope of protection to
previous members of sports teams at institutions of higher education
who never signed a professional sports services contract with a professional sports team.[8]

The impact of these statutes remains to be seen. Early indications
show that many sports agents are ignoring the statute certification
requirements. One explanation for this is the pervasive lack of enforcement. Many prominent sports agents have disregarded the registration
process entirely. In 1989, San Francisco attorney Edward King maintained that "one of the most famous football agents in California has
not registered as an agent."[9] Apathy toward the lack of registration by
popular sports agents provides little incentive for the novice agent to
seek certification.

California exemplifies the effect non-enforcement of sports-agent-
specific statutes has on the certification procedure. Though California's certification program has existed for over eight years, the number
of registrants is strikingly low considering the volume of professional
and college teams and sports agents based in California.[10] One sports
agent candidly noted, "Most agents that I know have not registered
anywhere. If they have, it's been in their home state."

An additional explanation for the lack of sports-agent registration in
California and other states is the statutory language granting attorneys
licensed to practice in the state exemption from the provisions of the
statute.[11] Requiring all athlete representatives to register, including
licensed attorneys, would increase the number of registrants as well as
the state's ability to enforce the provisions of the statute effectively.

Texas has probably been the most aggressive with its statute thus far,
on December 22, 1989 fining an agent and a firm $10,000 each for
violation of its agent law.[12] Former Heisman Trophy winner Johnny
Rodgers and Total Economic Management of America, Inc. were accused of contacting the 1989 Heisman Trophy winner Andre Ware of
the University of Houston. In addition to the contacting violation, the
alleged violations included offering gifts, cash, and other inducements
to Ware's mother.[13]

According to Senator John Culver, the development of these state
rules "possibly constitutes an over-reaction to some of the more cele-
brated instances of abuse."[14] This overreaction is part of the reason
that laws have developed that cannot solve and are not solving the

problems. All the athlete/agent-specific statutes apply to any person engaging in athlete representation. Registration may be viewed as consent to be subject to jurisdiction in the state courts in the event of a violation of the statute. Iowa requires non-resident sports agents to file an irrevocable consent to service of process with the Secretary of State.[15] Most statutes, however, fail to provide similar guidelines explaining the jurisdiction of state courts for violations committed by unregistered and out-of-state sports agents.

The key distinction between the existing NCAA, ARPA, ABA, and union regulations and the new trend of athlete/agent-specific statutes is the ability of state regulators to impose civil and criminal sanctions for non-compliance with the provisions of the statute. The majority of the statutes provide for the imposition of both criminal and civil sanctions. While all the statutes provide civil sanctions, only Minnesota, Tennessee, and Georgia do not classify violations of the statute as criminal actions.

Many sports agents view the NCAA regulations as unenforceable and therefore routinely ignore their existence. In an attempt to rectify this problem, three states thus far have specifically incorporated the NCAA and/or NAIA[16] rules and regulations into their agent regulatory statute.[17] This procedure allows for the imposition of criminal or civil sanctions on sports agents who violate the rules governing intercollegiate sports.

Agent-specific laws supplement already-existing state statutes that have been applied on occasion to sports-agent activities. The prosecution of Richard Sorkin under New York State criminal laws in 1977 is one of the earliest examples of the prosecution of a sports agent under existing state laws. In 1989, prosecutors in Florida filed fraud and conspiracy charges against a Florida sports management firm. State criminal statutes are being asserted by various state prosecuting agencies. Former Atlanta agent Jim Abernethy was found guilty under a state statute covering tampering with a sporting event as well as commercial bribery and violation of deceptive trade law. The trial of the sports agent who represented Kevin Porter, a former Auburn University football star, led to a successful prosecution under state law in an Alabama county circuit court.[18] That conviction, however, was later reversed on appeal.

Federal Regulation

Although sports topics tend to generate a great deal of public and political interest, federal legislation in sports has been rare. At present there is no federal legislation specifically applicable to the sports agent.

(Federal legislation recently proposed is set forth in Appendix III.) Although it would seem that federal legislation might best serve the consumer student athlete, such legislation realistically may never occur. According to Senator John Culver, "The only reason people sponsor bills is if it will help them get elected." Culver maintains that the sports-agent issue is not enough of a "grabber" and consequently is not likely to result in legislation.[19]

As with state laws, however, several illegal activities may receive the scrutiny of federal authorities. Federal charges of mismanagement of funds, fraud, and racketeering were made in the Walters-Bloom trial. The prosecuting tool used in that trial and contemplated in others is the Racketeer Influenced and Corrupt Organizations Act, commonly referred to as RICO,[20] which is especially noted for the broad range of cases where is has been asserted by prosecutors. RICO was initially developed to attack organized crime and stop political corruption. Since 1970, when the RICO act first became law, its scope has recognized few boundaries. It has extended so far that some commentators, including members of Congress, have called for its power to be cut back.

The application of RICO to the early agent contracts with athletes understandably caught some commentators by surprise. The application of the RICO statute seems to refute those claims made by so many Walterses and Tropes about the inapplicability of NCAA rules. Walters and Trope were not alone in their belief. Lonn Trost, the head of the sports department at the national law firm of Shea & Gould, testified at the Walters-Bloom trial that he had told the agents that signing student athletes to contracts before their eligibility expired did not violate any criminal statutes.[21] Walters, Bloom, Trope, and Trost all turned out to be wrong.

What RICO does that is unique is create three new criminal offenses. If a party violates two or more of a list of approximately thirty criminal statutes over a period of ten years, he or she may be found guilty of acquiring, controlling, or operating an "enterprise" through "a pattern of racketeering activity." If the party is convicted, the penalty for the RICO violation alone is seizure and forfeiture of the assets from the illegal enterprise and a fine of up to $25,000. In addition, under RICO, not only can the government bring an action but the civil provisions also allow private citizens to bring actions and gives them the right to recover three times their actual damages and reasonable attorneys' fees.

Commentators in search of a more direct federal vehicle to regulate agents have set forth various types of sports-agent-specific legislation ranging from a federal version of some of the state legislation to a model based on federal securities law. In 1989 proposed legislation was being circulated by Congressman John Bryant of Texas. This legislation, set forth in Appendix III, closely resembles legislation proposed by the Sports Lawyers Association and Senator Robert Packwood in 1985. It would bring the regulation of sports agents under the authority of the Secretary of Commerce, and it addresses issues of agent competency, allows for character and skill investigations, and sets forth methods to revoke an agent's registration.

One other source of federal regulatory activity is the federal Securities and Exchange Commission. The SEC has reportedly exerted some of its regulatory authority in the sports-agent industry. According to Robert Ruxin in *An Athlete's Guide to Agents,* this agency has "reprimanded" some of the larger sports management firms for violating existing investment advisory laws.[22]

If federal legislation is not passed, we will be confronted with a melee of state statutes, augmented by whatever the NCAA, the leagues, and the players' unions can do to develop solutions for the agent regulation problems. As of 1989, only the players' unions had made some effort at ensuring agent competency. As Senator Culver points out, "The 'patch quilt' is just hopeless"; there is "no way to operate responsibly and honestly in that kind of environment."

Private Lawsuits

Private actions theoretically most often involve the athlete bringing a lawsuit against the sports agent.[23] The relationship between the athlete and the agent is based on general principles of agency and is formalized in what could be labeled as an agency agreement.[24] Thus, with some exceptions, general principles of contract and agency law apply to the sports agent/athlete relationship. The actions will most often be brought because the agent did not do something promised, or did something fraudulently or negligently. According to Edward King, the biggest problems once the athletes sign with agents involve "fraud and undisclosed kickbacks."[25]

King has encountered a number of unsavory situations where agents have simply put the athletes into their own bad deal. "Generally when the athlete comes to me, financially the agent has put him in the grave and he's looking up at the dirt that is piling up on top of him." King maintains that "every remedy that you need is now available via a private cause of action." King believes there is a lawsuit for every agent problem. The number of reported cases in this area is not large compared with the number of problems that reportedly occur. According to sports agent Reginald Turner, often these cases are settled before litigation occurs.[26] One reason for this is that often there are not funds remaining after the agent's wrongdoing occurs; so there is nothing for the injured athlete to pursue in a lawsuit.

Although the suit brought by an athlete against an agent is the most common, other actions may also take place. These include agents suing athletes for breaching their contract and agents suing agents for interfering with a contractual relationship. Some of the possible causes of action in each of these relationships are examined below.

Athlete v. Sports Agent

The law governing agency generally maintains that "agency is a consensual, fiduciary relation between two persons, created by law, which one, the principal, has a right to control the conduct of the agent, and the agent has a power to affect the legal relations of the principal."[27] The law of agency also generally maintains that an agent is liable for all damages that arise as a result of his or her legal actions. Thus, an athlete, the principal, who is damaged due to an action by the sports agent may pursue any applicable legal cause or action against the agent. Conversely, the athlete will generally be required to pay whatever amount is owed under the agency agreement if the agent is discharged prematurely.

The private action may be the only route by which the athlete can recover for improprieties regarding any contracts not related to playing. For example, none of the players' association regulations regulate any aspect of endorsement contracts. The same is true for the state acts. For many athletes, the endorsement contracts constitute a substantial portion of their annual income; for some, it exceeds their salaries.

A lawsuit for breach of contract, for failing to perform for the athlete as promised, is the most obvious action to be taken against an agent. The terms that a sports agent or athlete is obligated to comply with are generally set forth in the agency agreement—that is, the contract that sets forth the terms of their agreement. The sports agent is required to provide service in "good faith" to the best of his or her ability. This situation contrasts sharply with standard agency rules, which hold the agent to an industry standard, not to a good faith, best individual effort standard. Under this standard there is no obligation on the part of the agent to obtain the best contract possible.

Sports Agent v. Athlete

A sports agent may be most likely to bring an action against an athlete to recover payments due under that contract for sports-agent services performed. Such an action would constitute a basic action for breach of contract and would involve standard evidentiary issues of proof as to what the parties agreed to and what actually transpired.

A remedy that an agent might seek for breach of contract that is not likely to meet with any success is a suit by the agent for specific performance, forcing the athlete to honor the agency agreement, or for an injunction, barring the athlete from retaining any other agent. Both these remedies essentially seek to bind athletes to a relationship they do not desire to be in. The law generally will not enforce such agreements, particularly when the remedy at law, money damages, is adequate. It is only in the exceptional circumstance that the law will force parties to perform under the terms of a personal service contract. The law abhors forcing a personal relationship where money damages can resolve the dispute.

The remedies of specific performance, where a court orders the parties to perform under the terms of their contract, and the injunction, which would bar the athlete from signing a representation agreement with any other agent, are rarely awarded. These so-called "equitable" remedies are unique because they do, in a sense, conflict with an individual's personal freedoms.

A lawsuit by an agent against an athlete has some practical restraints as well. The lifeblood of the agent is the athlete client. A lawsuit by an agent, right or wrong, certainly will not be popular with the athlete community. Consequently, some agents maintain that it is best just to "let it go" and count the loss as a part of the business.

Even with this practical restraint in mind, sports agents do sue athletes. Agent Mike Trope may have been the most prolific litigator against student athletes. In the late 1970s he brought lawsuits against fourteen athletes drafted by the NFL, alleging that they all had broken contracts to be represented by him.[28] Trope based his actions on what became popularly known as an "offer sheet." In this scenario the student athlete would sign a contract while still playing for a college team. The catch, however, was that Trope would not accept the offer, by adding his signature, until after the athlete's collegiate eligibility was over. Trope's view was that this technique circumvented NCAA regulation against signing underclass students. The athletes that left him, their new agents, and the NCAA felt otherwise. Most of these lawsuits were settled out of court.[29]

In 1987 agent Norby Walters sued Brent Fullwood, a former Auburn University fullback, for failing to perform under a contract and to give back $4,000 loaned to him under that contract.[30] The loan and the signing had taken place before Fullwood completed his collegiate career at Auburn University.[31] The lawsuit was prompted by Fullwood hiring a different agent to represent him. In *Walters v. Fullwood* the judge, in denying the agent's action, stated that the loans violated NCAA rules and said, "We decline to serve as 'paymaster of the wages of crime, or referee between thieves.'"[32] Another interesting point about the *Walters v. Fullwood* case is that it is one of the first to put the force of law behind NCAA rules. The Walters-Bloom case, discussed previously, amplified this ruling. In any other context the court may have simply viewed the payments by Walters as a loan and ordered repayment.

In an earlier case, *Zinn v. Parrish,* the standard for damages in an athlete/agent dispute was established. In this case agent Leo Zinn sought to recover fees owed to him for providing contract-negotiation services.[33] After Zinn had negotiated several contracts for Parrish the athlete terminated Zinn's services. He further informed Zinn that he did not intend to pay the 10 percent commission he had contracted to pay. The court held that the athlete was obligated to pay the agent for the services performed while the parties were under contract.

Sports Agent v. Sports Agent

The intense competition among agents makes it not surprising that another possible action is interference with a contractual relationship, when one agent "steals" a client from another. A case illustrative of this type of action is *Roundball Enterprises v. Richardson.*[34] In that case an action was brought by Roundball Enterprises, an agency that represents athletes, against G. Patrick Healy, another agent, and Michael Ray Richardson, a professional basketball player then represented by Healy. The allegation by Roundball Enterprises was that Richardson owed fees for representation services Roundball had provided and that Healy had interfered with their contractual relationship.[35] Tortious actions of this nature are recognized due to the potential economic harm caused to the contracting party that is interfered with.[36]

A similar suit was filed in 1988 for "tortious interference with a contract." In that case, as *Sports Inc.* reported, New York based agent Irwin Weiner sued Atlanta based David Ware and Florida based Mel Levine, asserting that they had interfered with his existing contracts. Ware and Levine denied the interference. Weiner noted, "I'm fed up with this. This signing more than one agent is the worst I've ever seen."[37]

When agents are asked about suing each other many mention the necessity of establishing one's turf in the business. Where suing former clients may not be in the agent's best interest in the long run, establishing to competing agents that your clients are not to be tampered with does seem prudent.

Member Institution v. Sports Agent

The member institutions may be the entities most harmed by sports-agent improprieties. An institution may receive stiff sanctions from the

NCAA if a player is found to have a relationship with a sports agent in violation of NCAA rules. Basically, as the NCAA has no direct contractual relationship with student athletes, it enforces its regulations by taking action against its member institutions. Curiously, the member institutions themselves do not generally have rules in place regarding sports agents. Much like the NCAA, they simply do not have the force of law behind them to enforce any regulations. The institutions are left to rely on private causes of action. A cause of action that may prove effective for member institutions against sports agents is interference with a contractual relationship. A number of cases have addressed the issue of a contractual relationship between the student athlete and a member institution and maintained that such a relationship may exist.[38]

Probably the clearest example of financial harm caused by a student athlete's dealings with a sports agent occurred with the University of Alabama. That member institution was required to forfeit $253,477 for using two ineligible players in the 1987 NCAA basketball tournament.[39] The players were declared ineligible because of their dealings with sports agents. It is widely felt that the school would not have had to forfeit the funds or lose the players had it not been for interference by the sports agent. Some state statutes are setting forth this type of lawsuit as a statutory cause of action.[40]

A few universities are taking a more active role in the agent-selection process. Some have ad hoc systems where coaches or administrators assist the athletes in their selection. Others, such as Temple University, have formal agent-screening committees. Dr. Michael Jackson, the head of the school's Sports Management Program, heads up the committee at Temple.

This chapter has set forth the primary laws that are in place to regulate agents. As we saw, any illegal activity that occurs can be prosecuted under existing state or federal laws. Those areas that regulators are finding most difficult to address are those that conflict with this country's long-standing views of amateurism. Coupled with this is our business ethic against paying someone to do business in a manner that, some say, resembles an old-fashioned bribe. The next chapter examines amateurism and how what some refer to as myths are finding their way into state laws and clouding the issues that should be addressed in reforming the sports-agent industry.

Chapter 5

The Last Amateurs on Earth: Amateurism and Opportunity

"Ancient Amateurism is a myth."[1]

Many of the controversies surrounding the amateurism issue revolve around how the term "amateur" should be defined. It may be impossible to present a general definition. In simplest terms, an amateur is whatever the organization regulating the particular athletic event or organization says it is.[2] This definition generally appears in the organization's constitution or bylaws. Most popularly, an amateur is defined as someone who participates, and always has participated, in sports solely for pleasure and for the physical, mental, or social benefits. The amateur receives no financial gain of any kind, direct or indirect, for his or her athletic prowess.

The payment of any money to amateur athletes has traditionally been viewed as contradicting the true meaning of amateurism.[3] It is when some sort of payment is made that questions of amateurism are raised. Under NCAA rules, of course, any such payment is not allowed. Often "boosters," alumni, and the schools themselves "cheat," however, by making payments to student athletes when it is advantageous for them to do so. The cheating sometimes takes the form of a monetary payment, or sometimes is made in goods or services. Some agents also cheat, seeking an advantage as well, by paying student athletes to sign representation agreements with them.

There is some sense to the logic that says that if NCAA member institutions are allowed to pay athletes, the agents, boosters, alumni, and other potential cheaters will not. At a minimum, some of the opportunity to cheat will be removed. NCAA Executive Director Richard Schultz, on the other hand, maintains that payments by schools would simply raise the ante for agents.

The technique of paying student athletes is particularly successful for student athletes from economically disadvantaged families. Ironically, NCAA rules prevent these student athletes, who receive scholarships, from working. They are thus forced to ask their families for extra money in order to pay for anything from clothes to a date to a stereo system like the student's in the dorm room next door. If an athlete's parents cannot afford the expenditure, the athlete may be tempted to look elsewhere. Often a willing donor is the sports agent, booster, or alumnus. Such payments are presently against NCAA rules and many state laws. Yet it is important to understand why the payments take place and how the apparent demand for these payments may be reduced.

Coupled with the issue of money is a general view that, unlike their professional counterparts, amateur athletes participate in sports for the glory of the sport alone. Both the pay and the motive issues are commonly viewed as having originated in ancient Greek athletics. But we shall see that this interpretation is questionable at best: as David Young has remarked, "Ancient amateurism is a myth." The next sections will look at the origins of rules against compensation to amateur athletes.

Origin of Rules Against Compensation

The Ancient Greeks

Amateurism in sports is commonly posited on the Olympic model, which in turn is assumed to derive from ancient Greek athletics. The "myth" of ancient amateurism is that there was some society, presumably the Greeks, in which athletes participated in sport solely for the glory and received no compensation for their participation or winning. This view is found in one of the most extensive studies of the relationship of college athletics to the university as a whole, which was conducted by the Carnegie Foundation in 1929 and published in *American College Athletics* by Howard J. Savage.[4] According to this view, Savage writes, "The essential differences between the amateur and the professional in athletics were clearly understood among the ancient Greeks."[5] Classicist David C. Young, however, in his book *The Olympic Myth of Greek Amateur Athletics*, writes that he "can find no mention of amateurism in Greek sources, no reference to amateur athletes—no evidence that the concept 'amateurism' was even known in antiquity. The truth is that 'amateur' is one thing for which the ancient Greeks never even had a word."[6] In fact, Young traces the various levels of compensation that were received in ancient times and uncovers a prize in one event that was equal to ten years' wages.[7]

The absence of compensation was not an essential element of Greek athletics.[8] As another classicist notes, the ancient Greeks "had no known restrictions on granting awards to athletes."[9] Many athletes were generously rewarded; according to Young, the only real disagree-

TABLE 1 Athletic Events

		Prize (in amphoras of oil)	Drachma Value (12 drachmas per amphora)	Number of Days' Wages (at 1.417 drachmas per day, skilled)	Number of Years' Full Employment (at 300 days)
Stade*					
men	first	100	1,200	847	2.82
	second	20	240	169	.56
youths	first	60	720	508	1.69
	second	12	144	102	.34
boys	first	50	600	423	1.43
	second	10	120	85	.28
Pentathlon					
men	first	60	720	508	1.69
	second	12	144	102	.34
youths	first	40	480	339	1.13
	second	8	96	68	.23
boys	first	30	360	254	.85
	second	6	72	51	.17
Wrestling					
men	first	60	720	508	1.69
	second	12	144	102	.34
youths	first	40	480	339	1.13
	second	8	96	68	.23
boys	first	30	360	254	.85
	second	6	72	51	.17
Boxing					
men	first	60	720	508	1.69
	second	12	144	102	.34
youths	first	40	480	339	1.13
	second	8	96	68	.23
boys	first	30	360	254	.85
	second	6	72	51	.17

*A sprint of approximately 200 meters.
Source: David C. Young, *The Olympic Myth of Greek Amateur Athletics* (Chicago: Ares, 1985), pp. 119–120.

ment among classical scholars is when these payments or awards to athletes began.[10] Table 1 presents Young's figures showing the relative value of the prizes received by ancient Greeks in athletic competition.[11]

The myth regarding ancient Greek athletics apparently was developed and perpetuated by individuals who profited in various ways from the development of such a system.[12] Young examines the work of the scholars who are most often cited for espousing these views of Greek amateurism. He cites an article written by classical scholar Paul Shorey in *The Forum* as one of the first misstatements of the actual history:

And here lies the chief, if somewhat obvious, lesson that our modern athletes have to learn from Olympia, if they would not remain barbarians in spirit. . . . They must *strive*, like the young heroes of Pindar, *only* for the complete development of their manhood, and their sole prizes must be the conscious delight in the exercise . . . and some simple symbol of honor. They must not prostitute the vigor of their youth for gold, directly or indirectly. . . . [T]he commercial spirit . . . is fatal, as the Greeks learned in their *degenerate* days. . . . Where money is the stake men will inevitably tend to rate the end above the means, or rather to misconceive the true end . . . the professional will *usurp the place of the amateur.* [Emphasis Young's][14]

This passage was written prior to the first modern Olympiad held in Athens in 1896 and was directed at potential Olympians. Young points out that Shorey writes about "the Greek record for the high jump" although there was no high jump at the time,[15] that the statements attributed to Pindar throughout the text do not exist,[16] that dates are off by five hundred years,[17] and that Shorey actually knew very little about Greek athletics.[18] Young goes on to cite other scholars with similar faults and shows that these scholars inevitably cited each other for authority.[19] One scholar, Harold Harris, in his *Greek Athletes and Athletics*, actually created an account of an ancient Greek athlete with detailed dates that Young concludes is a "sham" and "outright historical fiction"[20] and was probably designed to serve as "a moral lesson to modern man."[21]

The "modern man" for whom the lesson was apparently designed seems to have been the gentleman amateur athlete of Victorian England:

Harris' bogus Greek athlete and Shorey's false history of ancient athletics are not isolated cases nor mere instances of sloppy scholarship. They are representative examples of a far-flung and amazingly successful deception, a kind of historical hoax, in which scholar joined hands with sportsman and administrator so as to mislead the public and influence modern sporting life. We shall never know whether these men performed their deception consciously or unconsciously, nor does it much matter now. But the deception itself is still with us, and we need to inquire into its results and its causes.[22]

In simplest terms, Harris, Shorey, and other early scholars of Greek "amateurism" were part of a justification process for an elite British

athletic system that was to find its way into American collegiate athletics. The fact that scholars were promulgating these definitions of
amateurism meant that non-scholars would inevitably do so too. Probably the leading voice in the United States in favor of segregating pay
and amateurism was Avery Brundage, former president of the United
States Olympic Committee and the International Olympic Committee.
Brundage was one of the main opponents of Jim Thorpe's recovering
his Olympic medals, which were taken away because he had played
semiprofessional baseball. One of the ironies of Thorpe's losing his
medals was his statement that "I did not play for the money there was
in it, but because I liked to play ball."[23] Other athletes assumed false
names while playing semiprofessional baseball; Thorpe did not even
realize he was jeopardizing his eligibility.[24] Similarly, during Brundage's reign, Olympic hurdler Lee Calhoun lost his amateur status
because he received wedding gifts as part of his appearance on the
television show "Bride and Groom."[25]

Brundage's view of Olympic amateurism was published in an article
entitled "Why The Olympic Games":

The ancient Olympic Games . . . were strictly amateur . . . and for many cen-
turies, as long as they continued amateur, they grew in importance and sig-
nificance. . . . Gradually, however, abuses and excesses developed. . . . Cities
tried to demonstrate their superiority . . . by establishing special training
camps . . . , by recruiting athletes from other communities, and by subsidizing
competitors. Special prizes and awards and all sorts of inducements were
offered and winners were even given pensions for life. What was originally fun,
recreation, a diversion, and a pastime became a business. . . . The Games de-
generated, lost their purity and high idealism, and were finally abolished. . . .
[S]port must be for sport's sake.[26]

Brundage firmly opposed amateurs receiving any profit whatsoever
and justified his position with the Greek amateur athletic story. He took
many extraordinary steps during his term in power.

England

Young and other scholars contend that it was not the Greeks who
developed the current collegiate ethic of amateurism but scholars like
Savage and Harris as well as the Avery Brundages of the day and the
practices that developed in Victorian England. In fact, the first published definition of the term "amateur" by a sports organization was
made by the Amateur Athletic Club of England in 1866.[27] That definition stated that an amateur was:

Any gentleman who has never competed in an open competition, or for public
money, or for admission money, or with professionals for a prize, public money

or admission money, and who has never at any period of his life taught or assisted in the pursuit of athletic exercises as a means of livelihood; nor is a mechanic, artisan, or labourer.[28]

The purpose of the Amateur Athletic Club was to give English gentlemen the opportunity to compete against each other without having to compete with professionals.[29] The development of concepts of amateurism in Britain were largely based on class distinctions. The distinctions were forced by the uses of so-called "mechanics clauses" in amateur definitions, like the one quoted above, which maintained that mechanics, artisans, and laborers could not participate in sports as amateurs.[30] According to Ronald A. Smith, in his book *Sports and Freedom,* the British Amateur Rowing Association had such a clause in its eligibility rules in 1870.[31] It was from these rules that the modern eligibility rules of the NCAA evolved. In fact, any negative connotations that remain today regarding professionalism probably evolved from this distinction. Interestingly, part of the reason for the "mechanics clause" was that those who used their muscles as part of their employment in fact had a competitive advantage.[32]

United States

Smith describes the profound amateur/professional dilemma that confronts American universities in this way:

If a college has truly amateur sport, it will lose prestige as it loses contests; if a college acknowledges outright professional sport, the college will lose respectability as a middle-class or upper-class institution. The unsatisfactory solution to the dilemma has been to claim amateurism to the world, while in fact accepting a professional mode of operation.[33]

The first two sports to face these questions of professionalism versus amateurism in the United States were baseball and rowing. Initially, the norm in sports in this country was professionalism. Baseball was played at the semiprofessional level as early as 1860, and the first professional team, the Cincinnati Red Stockings, was formed in 1868,[34] the same year in which the New York Athletic Club, the first amateur organization in the United States, was formed.[35]

"Professionalism" in college sports abounded. For example, in the 1850s Harvard University students rowed in a meet that had a $100 first prize purse, and in the 1860s they raced for as much as $500.[36] Smith maintains that amateurism as historically conceived was largely absent from college sports at the beginning of the twentieth century:

By the early twentieth century, there was probably no college in America which was able to preserve amateurism in men's sport, as competition for money and non-money prizes, contests against professionals, collection of gate receipts, support for training tables, provision for athletic tutors, recruitment and payment of athletes, and the hiring of professional coaches pervaded the intercollegiate athletic scene. Professionalism had invaded college sports and had defeated amateurism as it was understood in the nineteenth century.[37]

One of the more graphic illustrations of the benefits students received, even in the early 1900s, involved 1904 Yale football team captain James Hogan. After the final game in his career Yale rewarded Hogan by sending him to Havana on vacation.[38]

One reason that sports in colleges developed beyond amateurism in the United States as opposed to its British counterpart was the sheer number of competing institutions.[39] In England upper level education meant Oxford or Cambridge. With only two institutions the odds of stepping outside the established bounds of amateurism were not that high. In the Untied States, on the other hand, even early on, the Ivy League schools competed strongly against each other in sports. And not only were there private institutions but also public colleges and universities.[40] Even if Harvard and Yale wanted to be the athletic and intellectual elite of the United States, as Oxford and Cambridge were in England, they could not do so. As Smith notes, with the Wesleyans, Cornells, and others developing athletically, refusing to compete against them would cause Harvard and Yale to lose their athletic "esteem and prestige."[41] According to scholars like Smith and Daniel L. Boorstin, the English system of amateurism, loosely derived from the Greeks, simply did not have a chance of working in the United States.

Competition among a larger number of institutions certainly was a major element in the weakening of Victorian notions of amateurism. Another is what Smith refers to as a difference in egalitarian beliefs:

The English amateur system, based upon participation by the social and economic elite and rejection of those beneath them from participating, would never gain a foothold in American college athletics. There was too much competition, too strong a belief in merit over heredity, too abundant an ideology of freedom of opportunity for the amateur ideal to succeed. . . . It may be that amateur athletics at a high level of expertise can only exist in a society dominated by upper-class elitists.[42]

Even with this sort of ideological conflict, the NCAA's early years were heavily burdened by attempts to enforce various amateur standards.

In spite of this tradition, or perhaps because of it, in 1909 the NCAA, through its committee on amateur law, recommended and later adopted the following amateur/professional distinction:

1. An amateur in athletics is one who enters and takes part in athletic contests purely in obedience to the play impulses or for the satisfaction of purely play motives and for the exercise, training, and social pleasure derived. The natural or primary attitude of mind in play determines amateurism.

2. A professional in athletics is one who enters or takes part in any athletic contest from any other motive than the satisfaction of pure play impulses, or for the exercise, training or social pleasures derived, or one who desires and secures from his skill or who accepts of spectators, partisans or other interests, any material or economic advantage or reward.[43]

With this, Victorian England's amateur/professional distinction was incorporated into American collegiate athletics.

The first eligibility code basically sought to ensure that the athletes who participated in collegiate sports were in fact full-time registered students who had not been and were not being paid for their participation in athletics. The first (1906) NCAA Eligibility Code is set forth below:

The following rules . . . are suggested as a minimum:

1. No student shall represent a college or university in any intercollegiate game or contest, who is not taking a full schedule of work as prescribed in the catalogue of the institution.

2. No student shall represent a college or university . . . who has at any time received, either directly or indirectly, money, or any other consideration, to play on any team, or . . . who has competed for a money prize or portion of gate money in any contest, or who has competed for any prize against a professional.

3. No student shall represent a college or university . . . who is paid or received, directly or indirectly, any money, or financial concession, or emolument as past or present compensation for, or as prior consideration or inducement to play in, or enter any athletic contest, whether the said remuneration be received from, or paid by, or at the instance of any organization, committee or faculty of such college or university, or any individual whatever.

4. No student shall represent a college or university . . . who has participated in intercollegiate games or contest during four previous years.

5. No student who has been registered as a member of any other college or university shall participate in any intercollegiate game or contest until he shall have been a student of the institution which he represents at least one college year.

6. Candidates for positions on athletic teams shall be required to fill out cards, which shall be placed on file, giving a full statement of their previous athletic records.[44]

This initial set of amateur guidelines was largely ignored by the member institutions.

At various times after the establishment of this code the NCAA sought to define its views on amateurism further. An intermediate step was formally to adopt the Amateur Code into the NCAA Constitution.[45] This step, said Palmer E. Pierce, president of the NCAA, was intended "to enunciate more clearly [the NCAA's] purposes; to incorporate the amateur definition and principles of amateur spirit; [and] to widen the scope of government."[46] As the monetary strength of the NCAA grew, so too did its power to enforce the principles of amateurism it incorporated into its constitution.

The same basic problem that inspires institutions to cheat in various ways today existed even in the formative years of collegiate sports. A winning collegiate athletic program had the potential to bring high revenues to the institution. In 1903, Yale University, which was then a national football power, made $105,000 from its football program.[47] This type of financial incentive, then as well as now, may well cause a school to cheat to obtain the best talent.

The revenue sources available to member institutions increased with the advent of television and radio. With this came increased incentives to violate NCAA amateur standards regarding recruitment and payments to student athletes. In response, in 1947 a so-called "Sanity Code" was adopted by the NCAA. The code restricted athletic scholarships to those based on need only.[48] The goal of the code was to stop the unbridled spending by member institutions to recruit and retain student athletes. Almost immediately seven institutions violated the code and were brought up for suspension under the association's rules; in addition to these seven it was suspected that twenty others had violated the rules as well.[49] At their 1950 convention the membership did not cast the two-thirds majority vote necessary to suspend these seven. Not surprisingly, two years later the Sanity Code was dropped and scholarships were again based on athletic prowess alone.

The pressures to succeed athletically provided the incentive for institutions to cheat, even at the risk of suspension. When the opportunity came to enforce the rules the association would not do so. But even given the problems of lack of member support throughout its development, the NCAA continues to bar compensation to student athletes above room, board, tuition, and educational fees. To understand the changing role of the NCAA one must clearly understand its history. It began as an organization, formed at the urging of a President, to promote safety in athletics. The flowery tales of Greek amateurism are not a part of that foundation. But it is those visions of some sort of pure amateurism that seem to bar some changes that should take place within the structure of college sports. This organization formed to promote safety is now the largest amateur sports organization in existence that still prohibits its athlete members from receiving any adequate compensation through legitimate means.

Against this historical backdrop, the reality is made clearer: the system's lack of compensation permeates virtually all decisions that are made regarding collegiate athletes today. The NCAA is not the only source of this "no-pay" spirit. Another example is a Federal District Court judge's ruling in *Walters and Bloom v. Fullwood and Kickliter.*[50] Although the primary issue in that case was which entity had jurisdiction or the power to decide the dispute between the parties, Chief Judge Charles L. Brieant found it appropriate to state his views on amateurism. In his conclusion, referring to what must appropriately be called a stereotypical view of amateurism, Brieant wrote:

All parties to this action should recognize that they are the beneficiaries of a system built on the trust of millions of people who, with stubborn innocence, adhere to the Olympic ideal, viewing amateur sports as a commitment to competition for its own sake.[51]

In his opinion Brieant cited other scholars who disagreed with Young's view and maintained that Greek tradition excluded compensation.[52] Certainly the ultimate decision in the *Walters and Bloom v. Fullwood and Kickliter* case may be appropriate. But it seems problematic to base that decision on perceived Greek ideals that, as we have seen, may be incorrect. In fact, Young would probably maintain that they are not only incorrect but unfair as well. Young said that he wrote his book on amateurism because he "couldn't stand to see all these problems associated with amateurism blamed on all those poor dead Greeks."

The Athlete's View

Like Smith, Allen Sack of the University of New Haven also emphasizes that this sort of professional-amateur hybrid is unique to American collegiate sports.[53] Between 1983 and 1985 the Center for Athletes' Rights and Education conducted a study of the experiences of collegiate athletes.[54] The study sampled 644 student athletes at 47 colleges and universities. One segment of that study dealt with student athletes and some of their perceptions regarding amateurism and compensation.

One question asked in the survey was whether it was wrong to accept monetary payments "under the table" for traveling, living expenses, and other expenditures;[55] 42 percent of those surveyed saw nothing wrong with it.[56] The survey also asked whether the athletes felt they deserved a share of the television revenues that they generate for their universities; 43 percent felt that they did.[57] In response to a question that examined the motive issue for participation, a long-standing element of the amateur definition, 40 percent of Division I student athletes[58] and 81 percent of Division III athletes said they participated for the "fun of it."[59] Interestingly, Division III does not generate the same level of income or have the same level of competition as Division I.

One other interesting statistic uncovered by Sack's survey is that 69 percent of the Division I athletes felt that they were adequately rewarded for their time and effort in being involved with college sports. Sack views this figure with some skepticism:

> In most instances, athletes probably view an athletic scholarship as adequate payment for their services. Athletes who need an added incentive often have access to an underground payment system which uses wealthy alumni to funnel money to athletes. By calling athletic scholarships "unearned" financial aid, and by forcing other cash payments underground, the NCAA has been able to protect the myth of amateurism.[60]

In 1989 Sack released another study that looked specifically at which athletes were receiving payments.[61] Sack invited a total of 3,500 active and retired NFL athletes to participate in his study. The 1,182 who returned his questionnaire represented 34 percent of the total group contacted. He sent 1,700 questionnaires to active players, of which 408, or 24 percent, were returned. He attributes this low rate to the fact that "the questionnaire contained some very sensitive questions and . . . the survey was conducted at a time when sports agents and professional athletes were being investigated by the F.B.I. for offering and accepting improper benefits."[62] As Table 2 indicates, Sack found that nearly one-third of the group admitted to having received payments in violation of NCAA rules, primarily from alumni but also from coaches and from the sale of game tickets.[63]

Perhaps more important than the number of players who took payments is the fact that 71 percent of the respondents said that the financial aid they received was inadequate and 78 percent said that they felt they deserved greater compensation than allowed by the NCAA. This was a 9 percent increase from the earlier survey. Among younger athletes, the percentage was 85 percent.[64]

Sack also looked specifically at the percentages of student athletes who were offered improper benefits by agents (Table 3). Of the athletes surveyed, 17 percent admitted receiving offers. The number of offers, as might be expected, increased with the talents of the individual athlete. When Sack looked at student athletes who had been recruited out of high school by fifty or more schools, the number increased to 31 percent. Of black student athletes recruited by fifty or more schools 63 percent had received offers. This is not surprising when one considers

TABLE 2 Players Who Knew Athletes at Their Colleges Who Took Under-the-Table Payments or Who Admitted Taking Such Payments Themselves

	Knew Others Who Took Payments		Admitted Taking Payments	
Conference	Respondents	%	Respondents	%
Southeast	115	67	115	52
Big Eight	76	60	75	35
Southwest	78	58	78	40
Pac-10	131	59	130	39
Big Ten	160	48	159	36
Independent	222	45	222	27
Western Athletic	51	43	51	31
Atlantic Coast	59	32	57	19
Other	197	25	195	13
TOTAL	1,089	48	1,082	31

Source: "Illicit Pay in Wide Use, Study Contends," *New York Times*, Nov. 17, 1989, A-33, col. 2; Allen L. Sack, "The Underground Economy of a College Sport," paper presented at the Joint Meetings of the North American Society for the Sociology of Sport and the Philosophic Society for the Study of Sport, Washington, D.C., Nov. 10, 1989.

the generally lower economic status of black student athletes and, therefore, their increased susceptibility to offers by sports agents.[65] Of Sack's black respondents, 48 percent were from what he defined as lower-income backgrounds, as opposed to 31 percent of the whites.[66]

In simplest terms the system of amateurism in the United States has evolved around the ethic that, particularly at the collegiate level, the person who plays the sport for fun is somehow purer than the one who earns an income from it or, worse yet, makes a living at it. Sack's studies show that there is a great deal of conflict over this view among student athletes.

Trust Funds

Outside the NCAA there are amateur entities that allow athletes to receive greater levels of compensation. Athletes involved in non-NCAA track and field are allowed to be paid appearance and endorsement fees, provided any money received beyond their actual travel and living expenses is maintained in a trust fund. Professional athletes are now allowed to participate in the Olympics at all levels, including millionaire professional tennis stars.[67] In the 1988 Olympics it was reported that some countries paid their athletes cash bonuses if the athletes won medals.[68] Allowing these payments to take place, of course, has not gone without criticism.

TABLE 3 Players Who Received Offers from Agents of Improper Benefits

No. of colleges recruiting the athlete	Black Respondents	%	White Respondents	%	Total Respondents	%
50+	43	63	94	17	137	31
20–49	39	39	108	17	147	22
0–19	133	32	265	8	398	16
Total	215	40	467	12	682	17

Source: "Illicit Pay in Wide Use, Study Contends," *New York Times*, Nov. 17, 1989, A-33, col. 2; Allen L. Sack, "The Underground Economy of a College Sport," paper presented at the Joint Meetings of the North American Society for the Sociology of Sport and the Philosophic Society for the Study of Sport, Washington, D.C., Nov. 10, 1989.

Probably the most visible "paid" amateurs are the track and field athletes. In the United States, The Athletics Congress, popularly referred to as TAC, regulates what amateur track and field athletes may receive. TAC also establishes regulations for trust funds which athletes may set up. They are allowed to put appearance monies and endorsement revenues into their TACTRUST fund. The TACTRUST rules set forth eleven specific reasons funds can be withdrawn from the account, including training and competition costs, health care, and agents' commissions.[69] The TACTRUST Agreement is set forth in Appendix IV.

This type of fund has been harshly criticized by a Canadian commission investigating amateur sports following the disqualification of Canadian sprinter Ben Johnson for the use of steroids in the 1988 Olympics. The *Sports Industry News* reports that Commission Chairman Charles Dugin referred to the trust funds as "pure subterfuge," noting that Johnson had been able to buy a $257,000 Ferrari and a $150,000 Porsche.[70]

Even sports that many view as the purest forms of amateurism provide compensation to athletes. A vivid example is the sport of fencing. As with many of the Olympic sports fencing has no professional level for the athlete to aspire to. Further, the training and travel expenses to participate at the amateur level are tremendous. Consequently, in August of 1988 the United States Fencing Association approved financial awards to the participants in the sport based on their performance in competitions.[71]

NCAA Pay Restrictions

In the light of these regulations, the irony of the NCAA rules becomes more obvious. Penn State football coach Joe Paterno put the contrast clearly in his autobiography, *Paterno: By the Book*:

Carl Lewis, a great track man, became a millionaire while remaining an amateur. All kinds of endorsement money was dumped on him, and all legal as long as the money was paid to a trust fund instead of directly to Lewis. That's legal in track, but not in football. Don't ask me why.[72]

The restrictions on payments to student athletes for their athletic abilities maintained by the NCAA extends even to endorsement opportunities and to outside employment.[73] The NCAA rule regarding payments to athletes states:

An individual loses amateur status through receipt of "pay," which includes, but is not limited to, the following practices:

(a) Educational expenses not permitted by the governing legislation of this Association;
(b) Any direct or indirect salary, gratuity or comparable compensation;
(c) Any division or split of surplus (bonuses, game receipts, etc.);
(d) Excessive or improper expenses, awards and benefits;
(e) Expenses received from an outside amateur sports team or organization in excess of actual and necessary travel, room and board expenses for practice and game competition;
(f) Actual and necessary expenses or any other form of compensation to participate in athletics competition (while not representing an educational institution) from a sponsor other than an individual upon whom the athlete is naturally or legally dependent or the nonprofessional organization that is sponsoring the competition;
(g) Payment to individual team members or individual competitors for unspecified or unitemized expenses beyond actual and necessary travel, room and board expenses for practice and competition;
(h) Expenses incurred or awards received by an individual that are prohibited by the rules governing an amateur, noncollegiate event in which the individual participates;
(i) Any payment, including actual and necessary expenses, conditioned on the individual's or team's place finish or performance or given on an incentive basis, or receipt of expenses in excess of the same reasonable amount for permissible expenses given to all individuals or team members involved in the competition;
(j) Educational expenses provided to an individual by an outside sports team or organization that are based in any degree upon the recipient's athletic ability, even if the funds are given to the institution to administer to the recipient;
(k) Cash, or the equivalent thereof (e.g., trust fund), as an award for participation in competition at any time, even if such an award is permitted under the rules governing an amateur, non-collegiate event in which the individual is participating. An award or a cash prize that an individual could not receive under NCAA legislation may not be forwarded in the individual's name to a different individual or agency;
(l) Preferential treatment, benefits or services (e.g., loans with deferred payback) because of the individual's athletic reputation or skill or pay-back potential as a professional athlete, unless such treatment, benefits or services are specifically permitted under NCAA legislation; and

(m) Receipt of a prize for participation (involving the utilization of athletic ability) in a member institution's promotional activity that is inconsistent with the provisions of 12.5 or official interpretations approved by the NCAA Council.[74]

The NCAA's employment rule presents a perfect "opportunity" for boosters, alumni, agents, or prospective agents to fill a gap for student athletes. The section governing outside employment maintains that an athlete on full athletic scholarship may not work during the school year or at any time that class is in session or, in the case of football, after practice begins.[75] The NCAA does this through bylaw 15.02.4, which limits the amount of financial aid a student may receive to "tuition and fees, room and board, and required course-related books."[76] The bylaws specifically include as sources of funds that must be considered in this amount "employment during semester or term time."[77]

The student athlete on full athletic scholarship may not be paid for athletic prowess and may not work for additional spending money. The throwback to the aristocratic idea of the amateur is clear here. If the student athlete has adequate funds for the activities of student life, the ideal situation is not to work. This clearly provides more time to concentrate on studies. However, if the athlete does not have the funds (from family or elsewhere) and may not work under the rules, what happens when the limited holiday earnings are gone, or, if the athlete desires to make a larger purchase, such as an automobile? Professors Lionel Sobel and John Weistart, among others, have noted how curious it is that students in drama, art, or computer science do not have to deal with this sort of rule. If they want to work, they can. If a philharmonic orchestra or a computer science firm wants to sign them on before they graduate, it can.

This discrepancy opens a window of opportunity that is often seized by boosters, alumni, or sports agents. Some people view payments in violation of NCAA rules as synonymous with other "victimless crimes." The athlete needs the money; no one is hurt in the transaction; the payment just happens to be against NCAA rules. In some states, of course, as well as potentially under federal racketeering laws, it is against the law. But former athlete agent Mike Trope probably spoke for many when he stated, "If I talk to a player and he needs a thousand dollars, I've got the money to give him."[78] One NCAA official noted that "Good agents abide by the rules, which only provide inroads for the unscrupulous agents. The good agents say it works to their disadvantage."[79] Paul Palmer, who admitted receiving payments from an agent, noted, "Some people did it for greed, some people out of need, I can't say I did it out of greed. If there was anything, it was more, toward need."[80]

Wall Street Journal columnist Frederick C. Klein has put the problem quite succinctly in an article entitled "College Football: Keeping 'em Barefoot." There Klein notes that "keeping the players the only amateurs in an otherwise thoroughly professional production merely encourages agent 'loans' and other shenanigans that occupy the sports-page headlines."[81] Klein's reference is to the obvious evolution that has taken place in college sports from a popular extracurricular activity to big entertainment—maybe, more appropriately, big, financially successful entertainment. Everyone involved in the enterprise is reaping cash benefits except the athlete.

Obviously the fact that the scholarship student athlete has the opportunity to receive an education, which is of great value, should not be ignored. The fact that the athlete receives no cash payment for being the linchpin of the lucrative entertainment enterprise, however, cannot be ignored either. The total receipts from the 1989 NCAA Division 1 basketball tournament were $66,300,000. Each team that made it to the tourney was guaranteed $250,200; if a team made it to the "final four" the figure was $1,251,000.[82] In 1989 the NCAA signed a contract with CBS to televise the basketball tournament for seven years for $1 billion. This will only add to the prosperity of the member institutions over the next seven years.[83] According to Phil Closius, "The student athletes are generating millions for the institutions. It's not fair for a kid like this not to have enough money to enjoy the college experience. Most kids get money from their parents. The kids from poor backgrounds can't get money from their parents."[84]

When we contemplate payments to athletes and why the NCAA should consider increased player compensation, two questions must be considered. The first is the pragmatic opportunity issue. If one accepts the fact that student athletes need funds, why should those funds not come from the member institutions rather than from boosters, alumni, or sports agents? Second, since student athletes are in fact the ones generating the funds, why should they not reap a greater share of the benefits?

Not all institutions are financially prosperous, of course; some lose money. This fact must be borne in mind in any analysis of increased compensation to the student athlete. Some institutions individually may not be able to foot the bill to provide the student athlete with more funds. A reallocation of the entire NCAA budget might remedy that problem.

II Changes

Chapter 6

Existing on Air? Pay, Employment, Loans, and Endorsements

If there is no foundation for the Greek ethic of amateurism, if there are funds available, if increasing compensation to student athletes would improve the condition of collegiate athletics, how should it be done? This chapter sets forth some of the major methods that could be used to increase the compensation that reaches the student athlete.

Pay

Paying the student athlete would be almost a natural progression from the long-time policy of paying coaches. The purest form of amateurism would have the athletes coach themselves or, in the extreme case, use graduate students as coaches, but certainly not paid professionals. According to Ronald A. Smith in *Sports and Freedom,* the professional coach has been a part of college athletics since 1864.[1] Moreover, even early on they earned more than most college professors and enjoyed greater visibility than the campus presidents.[2] Smith notes further that "intercollegiate athletics, almost from the first, had the professional spirit."[3] Today a salary above $100,000 is not uncommon for the successful college coach. In 1989 the basketball coach of the University of Nevada at Las Vegas, Jerry Tarkanian, earned a base salary of $173,855, received a percentage of the revenues from post-season championship competition and the use of a Cadillac, and had several other promotional and endorsement arrangements.[4]

The paid coach evolved in college athletics because the paid coach was able to win. The first professional coach, William Wood, was hired in 1864 to coach the Yale rowing team.[5] With Wood as coach Yale defeated Harvard in their dual championships for the first time.[6]

The term "paid amateur athlete" is no longer the oxymoron it was even a few years ago. No one would argue that the financial plight of the collegiate amateur athlete is not paradoxical. How can genuine financial problems of these athletes be remedied?

John F. Rooney, who has written two editions of the book *The Recruiting Game*, writes in the second edition in 1987, "I am now more convinced than I was in 1980, when *The Recruiting Game* was first published, that big-time collegiate sports must be either purified or professionalized."[7] Rooney's primary focus is on the recruiting methods used by the schools. However, he also considers athlete payments as a source of remedy. His "practical solution," however, goes beyond pay to separating the athletic and academic functions of educational institutions. Essentially Rooney would have sports simply use the facilities of the universities, with little affiliation otherwise.[8]

An attempt to bridge the gap to some degree has been made with the Pell Grant, which may be awarded to student athletes based on need.[9] The amount made available under the Pell Grant was recently raised from a $900 maximum per year to the 1989 level of $1,400.[10] The grant does represent a positive adjustment, as well as an acknowledgment of the problem, in regard to the financially needy student. It does not, however, take into account the plight of student athletes who are fortunate enough to have parents with a higher income level and who are therefore ineligible for any need-based grants. The most unfortunate bind to be in may be to have parents who earn a substantial income but choose not to give their child any money. There are parents who believe that all that is needed to attend school is provided by the athletic department. These student athletes are wholly dependent on their parents for spending money, but may actually receive nothing. Even if the student athlete wants to earn extra money independently, NCAA rules do not allow it.

The most extreme recommendations have called for student athletes to be paid an outright salary. The arguments for this approach generally maintain that college sports essentially serve as a farm system for the professional sports of football, baseball, and basketball. Furthermore, the argument continues, college sports earn millions for the institutions, millions that would not be earned except for the efforts of the student athletes. Economist Roger Noll of Stanford University provides an argument to support this position. He cites the case of John Paye, who was a star quarterback with the Cardinal in the 1980s. In his senior season Stanford had a record of eight wins and three losses and participated in the Gator Bowl. Noll notes that when Paye graduated, although many other star players remained, the Cardinal record fell to four wins and seven losses. Even with economic corrections for the site of home games and other factors Noll estimates that Stanford's net operating revenues declined by $400,000 the year after Paye departed. Yet Paye received a scholarship valued at only $17,000.[11]

Other economists, such as the University of Chicago's Gary Becker, view the NCAA as a cartel, an entity that "increases the profits of its members by assigning quotas that reduce production and raise prices."[12] As Becker observes, the members of the NCAA do this by "reducing competition for players, T.V. contracts, and tournaments."[13] In this way the members are able to maximize their profits without having to pay competitive wages. If student athletes are paid compensation, their wages will increase and profits for the member institutions will most likely decline.

One could argue that if the amount paid is substantial enough the athlete will not need any additional monies and much of the opportunity to bind the athlete to the agent contract with a cash payment would be removed. Given the circumstances surrounding athletic recruiting and the personal stake in winning that prevails in the coaching profession, it is not difficult to realize why cheating is so prevalent. In fact, it seems to many in the college athletic ranks that NCAA investigations and penalties are just the price of doing business. It has also become apparent that many athletes see college as a stepping stone to a professional sports career. Many of them have even grown to expect something extra for their "athletic services."

Of course, even with a high level of pay some athletes will still accept payments from agents; as Richard Schultz contends, the ante will just be raised. There may be a segment of athletes who will always accept the payments, as Paul Palmer has stated, not from "need" but from "greed." Edward King believes that athletes take payments because of egotism and that providing greater athlete compensation will have little or no effect on payments by agents.[14] "It has to do with bragging rights and ego massage. None of these guys take money because they're hungry. Most guys that took the money didn't need it."[15] It is not clear that there is a monetary solution for this segment of student athletes.

Anita DeFrantz, the president of the Amateur Athletic Foundation and a member of the International Olympic Committee, views participating in a revenue producing sport as "no different than a student job working on behalf of the university. In such instances, the athletes should be paid for what they do."[16] A collegiate and Olympic rower, DeFrantz recollects that "I was paid for serving breakfast and lunch in the infirmary." According to DeFrantz, with the pay they receive the athletes should be able to determine what classes they want to take, pay for them, and in other ways budget their time and funds. DeFrantz sees an additional benefit of making sports participation a paid activity that non-student athletes will not suffer from the belief that athletes are receiving "special treatment." The athletes will receive from the university only what they pay for.

In DeFrantz's view, to provide student athletes with a salary based on what they provide to the university and to allow athletes the discretion to spend the income on their education as time permits removes some of the illusory value of the athletic scholarship. "In this way they can pay for the education they want."

In support of this position, former collegiate and NFL star Reginald Wilkes says that the scholarship money he received while a student athlete at Georgia Tech "was gone right away. You pay the necessary expenses and try to do a few of the normal things in college life and it just runs out."[17] Apart from the need for more funds, Wilkes also feels that it is the student athletes who are making the real contribution to these programs, which are making millions of dollars from their efforts. "The athletes are putting themselves on the line physically and I think they should be paid somehow."[18] Wilkes, like others, is not sure what that "somehow" method should be. He says that one possibility is to set aside some sort of lifetime retirement or medical benefits plan."[19]

Nonetheless, the payment of an outright salary is probably not a method that will be adopted by collegiate sports reformers. Below are a few other reforms that might also be given serious consideration.

Stipends

Short of paying student athletes a full salary, a recommendation heard more and more is that all student athletes be eligible for a "student life" stipend. This stipend would provide an additional sum with every athletic scholarship to cover such activities as trips home or social activities. It would recognize that the average student requires more than room, board, tuition, and educational fees to have a normal student life. A stipend that at least brings the student athlete up to the same student lifestyle as the average student will prevent some students from taking payments from agents and remove the opportunity from some agents. Even Richard Schultz thinks a stipend may be appropriate, provided it is designed to bring the student athlete up to the same financial level as other students.[20]

Loans

If a student has truly pressing financial needs, a loan fund established by either the professional leagues or the NCAA might also provide an alternative source of funds. The professional leagues, in particular, are keenly aware of which college athletes have the highest earning potential. The leagues can use this knowledge to analyze the appropriateness of a given loan. The repayment could then later be deducted from the athlete's professional salary.

Although the NCAA will not have any control over the athletes once they become professional, a loan program from that entity would appear to sit better with them than the agent "loan program" that presently exists. The NCAA already allows student athletes to obtain bank loans to purchase career protecting disability insurance.[21] One reason why athletes were allowed to obtain bank loans for disability insurance was because agents were purchasing the insurance for student athletes as yet another client recruitment mechanism. This type of loan should certainly be more palatable to the student athlete than one from an agent, assuming the athlete has a clear understanding that all loans must be repaid, even the loan from the agent, either directly or in the agent's fee.

Employment

The final irony of the NCAA rules is that the athlete on full scholarship is generally not allowed to earn income from employment. The basic paternal goal of the NCAA is a good one: the student athlete should be spending time studying, not working. After practice, there is very little free time left for the athlete, and that time should be spent on the student's education.

What the rule also implies is that the student athlete does not know best how to utilize time, that is, an athlete allowed to work would do that instead of studying. The rule does not recognize that student athletes are not a homogeneous group requiring "paternal" guidance in all cases. A missing element in the NCAA system is some instruction to the student athlete on how to manage time. Assuming that takes place, the question of the athlete utilization of time becomes less of a concern. There are athletes who would not take payments from agents if they could earn the money themselves. NCAA rules, however, do not allow them to do so.

One other concern regarding athlete employment is the amount the athlete will be paid. Obviously the NCAA wants to avoid situations where the student athlete receives a hundred dollars an hour to shovel snow at Mojave Desert University from a university alumnus or athletic program booster. But this is a problem separate from the sports agent problem. The NCAA currently monitors this situation for summer employment and could do the same for employment during the school year as well.

One reason why rules allowing student athletes to work are not being passed by the NCAA is that the member institutions apparently do not trust each other. Each sees the other as Mojave Desert University. By not allowing employment at all, the institutions avoid the task of having to scrutinize jobs and wages.

Endorsements

Students might also be allowed to make paid endorsements under certain circumstances. At present the image and likeness of student athletes may be used by the member institution and booster clubs, but the athlete receives none of the revenue. Allowing endorsements would provide the student athlete with income while allowing the athlete to continue in school and play at the college level. Potential revenues for endorsements have increased tremendously. Former New York Giants football player Mel Hein told *Time* that "1938 was my big year. I got $150 for endorsing Mayflower Doughnuts. When I won the Most Valuable Player award, some pipe company sent me a set of pipes. Free!"[22]

The experience of Jarvis Redwine, an NFL running back, when he was playing for the University of Nebraska, illustrates the present inequities in the system. According to Redwine's former agent, Reginald Turner, a group of entrepreneurs wanted to use Redwine's image on posters, T-shirts, and figurines, seeking to capitalize on his athletic success and popularity. They contacted the university and were informed that that type of commercial activity could be done with teams but not with individuals. Contracting with individual athletes for endorsements was clearly in violation of NCAA rules. The businessmen went forward anyway and produced and sold some items with Redwine's image. When Redwine became aware of this, he wanted to receive compensation for the profit that was being made on him. When they declined, Redwine contacted Turner regarding enjoining them from further sales, and eventually the sales were halted. The normal remedy for such an action, of course, would be to recover for the value of the use of Redwine's image and likeness; ironically, NCAA rules would not allow an athlete to receive such an award. Redwine's story illustrates the fact that, as the situation stands now, team logos, pictures, names, and other identifying features can be sold for a profit, but the student athlete cannot be involved in any such transaction.

Another example of the use of an athlete's likeness and image where he receives no monetary benefit is the experience of La Salle University's Lionel Simmons. Simmons, a star player on the basketball team, decided not to leave school early to begin a professional basketball career, but to play his senior season. The university then ran an advertisement for the school featuring Simmons, which read, "It's hard to say how much money a La Salle degree is worth. But we know it's worth at least two million dollars."[23] The advertisement obviously used Simmons's likeness and image to attract students and therefore income to the school. Any other celebrity who was used probably would have been paid; Simmons was not.

Still another glaring example of endorsement rule contradictions involved former NCAA basketball star Steve Alford. Alford posed for a charity fund raising calendar. Because it was termed a commercial venture, he was suspended for violating NCAA rules. The rules have since been changed to allow such charity ventures.[24]

In direct contrast to student athletes' not being allowed to endorse products are the lucrative contracts the coaches in the college ranks are allowed to enter into. *USA Today* reported in 1986 that shoe endorsement income was a hefty part of a college basketball coach's salary: Rollie Massimino of Villanova earned $125,000 per year and Georgetown's John Thompson in excess of $100,000 from Nike. The article noted further that over seventy-five college coaches averaged $30,000 to $40,000 in shoe revenue per year.[25] Pam Lester, who was the general counsel for Advantage International, a sports management and marketing firm, and is now an attorney with a Washington, D.C. law firm, believes that "some schools are beginning to look at the large fees that basketball coaches receive under shoe contracts to the schools."[26]

A former longtime Stanford University representative to the NCAA, Jack Friedenthal, does not like the idea of student athlete endorsements. Friedenthal contends that, if such endorsements become common, "the beefcake industry will be really big."[27] He fears that producers of "Chippendales" calendars of collegiate athletes could become quite prevalent.

Endorsements, of course, are likely sources of income only for well-known athletes. According to Lester the endorsement market has shrunk throughout sports. This implies that it might take aggressive representation by a sports agent to get endorsements for even the most prominent collegiate athletes. The result could be the intervention of sports agents at levels never imagined. "It would open up a whole can of worms," Lester reflects, implying that somebody will find a way to pay even the unknown interior lineman as Friedenthal implies.

Bribes

An analysis of this area would not be complete without at least acknowledging why, beyond the amateurism aspects, American society looks down on payments made by individuals to induce another to do business with them. At some levels such payments are common and accepted. For example, incentives such as toasters or other appliances given to prospective customers by banks for the opening of new accounts are commonplace. So are the rebates offered by auto dealers. What we frown on are under-the-table payments.

The Foreign Corrupt Practices Act of 1977 epitomizes the problem from an American viewpoint. The act imposes U.S. concepts of morality on international transactions. The act was developed by the Securities and Exchange Commission to attack the perceived problem of U.S. corporations making payments to foreign officials in order to do business with their country. The response of U.S. multinationals to this restriction, as reported by *Newsweek,* was that it was too restrictive: "It's foolish not to offer a bribe if a bribe is expected."[28] To them, paying bribes in the international market, particularly in third world countries, was (is) just a way of doing business. Their further concern was that if the United States put in place a law barring its multinationals from making payments, multinationals from other countries would fill the void.

The concern is the same in the sports-agent business. If you enact a law declaring payments to induce student athletes to enter representation agreements illegal, those who continue to make the payments will have a business advantage. If you assume that the only people who will violate the law are unscrupulous individuals, then your assumptions are not unlike those of the Foreign Corrupt Practices Act: that the people (countries or agents) getting the business are those that are presumably not acting in the best interest of American society as a whole. An argument can be made that the market for agent or member institution incentive bonuses could be made aboveboard with payments made as in the banking and auto industries. In both of those industries it is clear that no party is going to offer much more than the competition. In the market for the student athlete the same type of settling may take place. If the incentives are "legalized" and they stabilize, as in the banking and automobile industries, then the student athlete may be in a position to make a decision based on the agent's ability, not on the size of the "signing bonus." A common retort to this is that, if an agent will bribe an athlete, the agent will also accept bribes from that athlete's team or elsewhere. Giving bribes says something about the agent's character.

Compensating the Student Athlete

Obviously there is much that is unfair about the level of compensation the student athlete receives. But to deny the issue altogether, as the

NCAA seems inclined to do, is unrealistic. For one thing, the foundation for the rules against compensation does not seem to truly exist. Various forms of compensation have long been a part of amateur sports. The Greek and the British models did not absolutely bar compensation; rather, social status seemed to be the controlling factor. Paul Lawrence, in his book *Unsportsmanlike Conduct,* writes that "many casual observers believe that the NCAA endorsed the participation of amateurs to keep intercollegiate athletics pure, but we cannot ignore the fact that it was cheaper to allow amateur rather than professional participation."[29] That factor must be considered as well.

Any increase in compensation to student athletes would constitute a major transition by the members of the NCAA. Such a transition, however, would not be without precedent. The adoption of the NCAA Sanity Code occurred largely because of the blatant disregard by member institutions of those rules that absolutely forbade subsidies.[30] Initially the Sanity Code required that these awards be made solely based on need. When the colleges disregarded this limitation in 1952, the member institutions voted that the awards could be based on athletic ability, without regard to need.[31] It appears that, once again, it is time to reevaluate the situation and increase compensation in some manner.

If direct payment to the student athlete is somehow too unpalatable, the NCAA might take some guidance from the Athletics Congress TACTRUST. In this way the student athlete could receive income in trust and receive a student life stipend, receive some other amount, or have access to it when the class graduates. Consideration could be given to using such an account as an incentive to graduate as well.

The level of compensation that student athletes are allowed to receive should be reevaluated, particularly in lieu of what Olympic amateur athletes are able to receive. Caution must be used by law and rule makers in second-guessing the needs and abilities of college athletes. College athletes often require more money than they receive under the rules, and there is no real reason why they should not receive it.

Chapter 7

Let Them Turn Pro? Underclassmen, the Professional Draft, and Education

Any incentive to a student to leave college prior to obtaining a degree should be weighed very carefully. To encourage student athletes to leave college early or to forego college altogether is certainly not desirable. One politician, Senator J. Bennett Johnston of Louisiana, is so strongly against athletes turning pro before their classes graduate that he has contemplated federal legislation to prevent it. Johnston stated, "It will ensure that they [athletes] at least finish school."[1]

But there will also be exceptional circumstances where the athlete, for financial reasons, needs to earn the income available from professional athletics at a younger age. It is not beyond the realm of possibility that such student athletes will return to receive their degree as others have, most notably basketball's Julius Erving. Should the leagues let them turn professional?

All the major sports now allow athletes to be drafted in various ways— before they enter college, while they are undergraduates, and when their class graduates.[2] The National Football League, however, had the longest standing policy against drafting anyone whose class has not graduated. Consequently, in recent years there was a new element thrown into the range of unscrupulous activities available to agents and student athletes. In general, it became clear that if a student athlete desired to become eligible for the NFL draft prior to his date of graduation, he only needed to violate an NCAA rule.[3] Once he did so, he was no longer eligible to participate at the collegiate level in that sport. This practice had been occurring most frequently in college football.[4]

Football and Basketball

The professional football and basketball leagues have both experienced the problems involved in trying not to draft players before their classes graduate. In football, once the student athlete is declared ineligible under NCAA rules, his only option (absent the successful development of a new competing or alternative league), if he desires to continue participating in the sport, is to join the NFL. The NFL did not normally allow undergraduates to enter the league until their class graduates, but it had a special "supplemental draft" that, at the NFL's option, allows an athlete to be drafted into the league in the event that he is declared ineligible.[5] The NFL's rationale for staying away from drafting underclassmen was generally attributed to the long-term relationship the NFL has had with college football.[6] In the 1940s and '50s the college game was much more popular than the professional version. The policy not to draft underclassmen was based primarily on trust by the college administrators that the NFL would not draft famous young collegians before their class graduated. As several cases demonstrated, however, it was possible to circumvent this agreement.[7] The beneficiaries of being declared ineligible were the student athlete and the sports agent. The student received a salary and the agent a percentage of the salary.[8]

The NFL was the only league with a policy of not drafting underclassmen,[9] and this policy was not and probably could not have been a formal one. The NFL made a determination that it would probably not be successful in court in enforcing its policy against drafting underclassmen. Several commentators have examined the issue and found that the rule would most likely be invalidated as a violation of the antitrust laws.[10] The league would probably be challenged with an antitrust lawsuit if it ever took the step to institute a formal rule against underclassmen entering their professional ranks. Basically, an antitrust action would argue that the NFL is the one place the underclassman can make a living from his football skills. By not allowing him to be drafted, so the argument would go, the NFL is conspiring against him, exerting its monopoly power, and not allowing him to make a living. This argument is extremely forceful, particularly in the absence of a competing league. The NBA's version of the same rule was found to be invalid several years ago in a suit brought by former NBA basketball player Spencer Haywood.[11] Following the suit, the NBA dropped its rule against drafting underclassmen, but since then only a small number of athletes have been drafted into the league before their classes graduated.[12]

Rarely does an athlete enter the professional leagues directly from high school. National Basketball Players Association Executive Director Charles Grantham is aware of only three such cases: Moses Malone, Bill Willoughby, and Darryl Dawkins. There is probably even less likelihood of an intake of undergraduate football players.[13] The general feeling is that to play football as a professional the physical maturity requirements are that much more stringent.[14] Gil Brandt, the director of player personnel for the Dallas Cowboys, told *Time* magazine in 1980 that "[Herschel] Walker and Earl Campbell are the only two players I've ever seen who could have gone straight from high school to the pros."[15] Dr. Clarence Shields and Dr. Donald Stevenson, sports medicine specialists in Los Angeles, indicate that physical growth required for professional football may not be achieved until about age twenty-two, approximately when the average college student graduates.[16] Stevenson indicates that a major factor is the level of training that the athlete has undergone, implying that, with more intense training, the athletes may attain the requisite physical maturity sooner. The most notable example of this early development is the NFL's Herschel Walker, who many, including Brandt, considered physically capable of entering the NFL after his freshman year at the University of Georgia.

By allowing underclassmen to apply to be drafted, the NFL has eliminated another opportunity for the unscrupulous agent to influence the athlete to do something "wrong" in order to pursue a professional career. Meanwhile, there is not a danger of a wholesale undergraduate exodus since most teams would still prefer to draft the more mature, better-trained graduates. The problem that still exists, however, is the need of the student athlete to renounce collegiate eligibility in order to enter the draft. The rule could be applied rather harshly in not allowing student athletes to change their minds, even if the initial application were made while the student athlete was under the influence of an unscrupulous agent.

The NCAA has had ongoing discussions recognizing that a student athlete should be able to explore his or her professional market value without being declared ineligible. In 1988 its Professional Sports Liaison Committee agreed to move forward with drafting legislation that would allow such student athletes to "test the market" and make an informed decision.[17] The rules, as they currently stand, make it difficult for a student athlete to gauge his or her value to the professionals without actually formally entering the draft. It is to be hoped that, as the NCAA continues discussions, the member institutions will work with the NFL regarding the problems athletes face in renouncing their collegiate eligibility.[18]

A major factor in making a determination to enter a professional draft is education. The student athlete must, in some way, receive unbiased counseling to make the decision to leave school early. That is why proper education and counseling become relevant not only about this decision but regarding the selection of an agent as well. A factor that makes this all the more important is the relative lack of success that those entering the NBA draft early have faced. According to a *Houston Chronicle* story, of 131 underclassmen who entered the draft between 1971 and 1987, only 20 percent bettered themselves by doing so, rather than waiting for their classes to graduate.[19]

Baseball and Hockey

Another tricky problem with NCAA rules is the eligibility of the prospective professional baseball or hockey player. Major league baseball has had little problem in the area of the draft, since its rules permit teams to draft players at the end of high school or after their junior and senior years in college; similarly, student athletes attending junior college may be drafted after either of the two years there. In the National Hockey League (NHL) athletes are eligible to be drafted at the age of eighteen; athletes can enter a supplemental draft if they are twenty years old or over, have never been drafted, and have spent at least one year in college. Student athletes in both of these sports may be drafted without the need to announce their availability, as is the case in football and basketball.

Being drafted in itself does not affect athletes' eligibility. The problem comes with negotiating the contract. Essentially, if the student athlete begins to negotiate a contract with a professional team, even if no agreement is reached, he loses his collegiate eligibility. NCAA rules allow him to receive an initial offer, but neither the student athlete nor a representative may negotiate from that point. If the athlete does continue to negotiate, then the professional team has a clear advantage in contract negotiations, since it knows that the athlete has jeopardized the only other alternative, remaining in college.

Education

The current system in all sports lacks a mechanism that allows a student athlete a method to fully explore his professional options. Former ten-year NBA veteran Len Elmore wrote:

I've seen a lot of friends get hurt. I care. Today young athletes have greater access to information than ever before, in the form of seminars for potential professional athletes and advice from former athletes on the pitfalls of poor agent-client relationships. Sadly, few take advantage of these opportunities.[20]

Probably the biggest cause of incompetent agents' being so successful in obtaining clients is that the incompetent agents are often the unscrupulous ones as well, the ones making the cash payments to student athletes to bind them as clients. Unscrupulous agents who are still able to obtain clients without the cash payments and have slipped through the cracks of any licensing procedure are probably successful because of the lack of information the student athlete is provided with about selecting an agent and the lack of opportunity to work with an agent prior to the expiration of collegiate eligibility. Harvard football coach Joe Restic has noted that "The only way [to control the agent tactics] is to allow players to sign early. But before you do, be sure they're educated, given the information they need."[21]

The point Restic raises is an interesting one in relation to the timing of student athlete/agent contacts. Penn State's football coach, Joe Paterno, has a similar view:

Why is it so terrible for a kid to talk with or even choose an agent who, within weeks, will negotiate for him with pro teams? I think all parties, including the kid, would be better off if we rethought the timing for freeing the player to talk or sign with an agent during his college career.[22]

Not allowing the early signing with an agent may interfere with the student athletes' negotiation with professional teams, and may thrust them into a situation they later wish to get out of.

For example, in baseball a student athlete may be drafted following his junior year in college. This athlete is not allowed to use the services of an agent to test the market. The team that drafts the player knows that once the student athlete has signed with an agent he cannot later change his mind and complete his senior year at college. This knowledge removes much of the negotiating leverage a college junior might have. It further removes the opportunity for the college junior to educate himself regarding his true market value.

Joe Paterno sees a similar dilemma in college football, where the NCAA rules limit the athlete's ability to change his mind even a short period of time after signing with an agent or a team:

If he should jump the gun he ought to have a grace period before his signature ends his eligibility. That breather would protect him against the plight of Herschel Walker, who, as a Georgia all-American, signed with an agent and accepted a handsome chunk of money. Then he woke up the next morning and said, "I think I did the wrong thing." In most states, even an ordinary consumer buying a vacuum cleaner on time is protected by a grace period.[23]

The lack of requirements for those entering the business as sports agents forces athletes to make their own evaluations of prospective agents' qualifications. The problem is that when the athletes seek advice from people they trust and they assume will give unbiased advice, they may find these sources to be acting out of self-interest as well. The coach is a likely source for advice, and that advice may not be without

bias. *Newsday* reported in 1988 that agent Lance Luchnick, who represented five first-round NBA picks in one year, made payments to
coaches to induce them to have their star athletes sign representation
agreements with him.[24]

The student athletes are not the only ones in need of education. If
student athletes must comply with NCAA rules to retain their eligibility, then the agents should be familiar with the rules so that they do
not risk the athletes' eligibility. Many agents do know the rules and
operate accordingly. However, the NFLPA certification meeting in
Washington, D.C. in 1989 left another impression. In a room of a few
hundred agents, the group was asked when they could initially contact
student athletes regarding representation and still be within NCAA
rules. Amazingly, no one appeared to know for sure. One person said,
"An hour after his eligibility expires"; another said, "Anytime, how else
could we operate?—as long as we don't sign them." The right answer to
the question is not important. Rather it is obvious that a large segment
of the agent population is unfamiliar with the eligibility rules for
student athletes.

The NCAA restricts student athletes from signing with an agent with
a rule that states:

An individual shall be ineligible for participation in an intercollegiate sport if
he or she ever has agreed (orally or in writing) to be represented by an agent
for the purpose of marketing his or her athletics ability or reputation in that
sport. Further, an agency contract not specifically limited in writing to a sport
or particular sports shall be deemed applicable to all sports and the individuals
shall be ineligible to participate in any sport.[25]

Obviously the rule does not stop the athlete from shopping for an
agent early, but it does forbid contracting. It is not clear what benefit, if
any, would come from allowing the student athlete to sign early. One
possible benefit would be to stop cheating, by making the early signings
aboveboard rather than encouraging the secret signings that take place
now. Bringing this activity into the open would provide an opportunity
for public criticism and scrutiny.

There is an obvious burden on not only the NCAA but the leagues
and the players' unions to disseminate information to athletes on the
quality of agents and, just as importantly, on the services that are
traditionally required by the athlete from the agent. The NCAA and
the players' associations can aggressively use their respective registration and certification programs to serve this purpose. The NCAA does
make available literature to aid the athlete in the selection of an agent,
including *A Career in Professional Sports: Guidelines That Make Dollars and
Sense.*[26] The NCAA can also require the athletic departments at the

member institutions to distribute information to student athletes regarding registered agents and also discuss the qualities and skills that may be desirable at a mandatory student athlete meeting. If necessary, the NCAA should consider using its sanction powers against member institutions that do not comply with a vigorous education program.

Similarly, the professional leagues and players' associations should take on the burden at initial rookie meetings or maybe even earlier at rookie tryout camps.[27] The unions should ensure that their members have as much information as the unions have about individual agents. With vigorous education programs in place student athletes should be better able to select competent agents and make decisions regarding turning professional before their classes graduate.

Charles Grantham says that the NBPA is talking with the NCAA and seeking ways to combine their education efforts. The NFLPA indicates that it has had similar conversations. When players' unions do make information on agents available it is not always utilized. According to Donald Fehr, the head of the MLBPA, "not as many as I would like" are taking advantage of the information the union has available for players.

Agent Screening Panels

Two other types of programs have shown some promise: those instituted by the individual NCAA member institutions and those instituted by individual professional teams.

Dick Schultz states that in 1989 only a "handful" of schools had instituted formal counseling programs.[28] Jack Friedenthal maintains that the panels are useful and can be used by the student athlete to gain all the information needed about agents well in advance of graduation. Friedenthal says, "It's a great solution. Not enough schools take advantage of it."[29] The schools that have put panels in place take different approaches within the NCAA guidelines. One of the most active panels is at Temple University in Philadelphia.

Temple University has established an agent screening panel not only to screen agents but to educate student athletes as well. The program received great attention when it was found that former Temple football star Paul Palmer had received payment from agents while still an undergraduate. Regarding Palmer and other student athletes who have accepted pay from agents, program head Dr. Michael Jackson says, "When the lure of money and security comes along, the student athletes are blinded. It's like love."[30] Temple University's program, particularly the one designed for its basketball players, is considered to be one of the country's most advanced. Jackson says that they began the screening of agents before the NCAA formally began encouraging its member institutions to conduct such programs.

The key members of the panel that aids student athletes in their selection of agents at Temple include Jackson, two law professors (one of whom is Temple's faculty representative to the NCAA), an assistant coach from the player's sport, and various outside consultants from insurance, legal, and other business disciplines.

Much of the counseling to the athletes is not unique. Often the goal is just to fill that void that Wilkes described, to help student athletes make what might be the most important business decisions of their lives. Jackson says the goal is to "try to advise the players not to make the typical mistakes."[31]

What is unique are some of the role-playing techniques Temple uses, complete with props and convincing performances—convincing to the extent that the athletes are not always sure where reality begins and role-playing ends.

In one session Jackson and his panel invited members of the basketball team to attend a meeting in a conference room to meet a prospective agent. At this special meeting one of the guest panelists, who was actually an agent, asked that year's star player, "What's the most money you've ever had?" While the student athlete was responding the panelist pulled out a briefcase with $20,000 and gave it to him. He then asked the athlete, "What else do you need?" The agent told the athlete, "Sign this representation agreement and you can have it . . . whatever it is." Jackson recalls that at this point the athlete asked him whether this was role-playing or the real thing. The agent then led the athlete outside to a new black Mercedes Benz sedan with his name stenciled on the side and handed him a set of keys with his name on the key chain. At this point one of the other athletes present urged the student athlete to sign with the agent. The agent then urged the athlete to drive the car around the track; while he was doing so a tape discussing the virtues of his representation services was played over the car's stereo system. Making the car available to the athlete had an added impact; the athlete had only had his driver's license for about a month. The panel at Temple had done their research.

After each exercise the athletes and panelists had the opportunity to discuss all the ramifications of the offers made. In the example above, even with the urging of teammates the student athlete ultimately did not sign the contract. Jackson says the success was a combination of the kid's desire to do the right thing and the fact that he did not undergo the pressure of a one-on-one sales pitch by the agent. Jackson adds that in some cases making offers of women and drugs can be instructive as well. He maintains that the role-playing and other education aspects of Temple's program have been successful. "If you walk up to some of our ball players and there's a chance you're an agent they probably won't shake hands with you."[32] Part of the strength of Temple's program for basketball players is their head coach, John Chaney. As the coach he has strict rules against team members speaking to agents under any circumstances prior to the expiration of their eligibility.

Other schools that have their own version of panels include Duke University, Baylor University, the University of Wyoming, and the University of Florida. The schools conduct their panels in different manners. For example, Duke does not become involved in the student athlete's selection process unless he requests them to. The University of Florida involves the athlete's parents in the panel process.

When Reginald Wilkes graduated from Georgia Tech there were no formal agent screening programs in place. "I wish there had been," Wilkes recalls. "The mechanisms just weren't there."[33] Jay Bilas, an athlete who had the benefit of a panel at Duke, expresses his satisfaction by stating, "I can't tell you how confident I felt making my final decision."[34]

Agent Craig Fenech has participated in a screening program as a prospective agent. Although he found the program theoretically sound, he points out that not all agents participate in it: "While I was following the established procedures, other agents were signing up athletes."[35]

Not everyone is enthusiastic about the panels. One critic is the president of the NCAA, Albert M. Witte of the University of Arkansas. His school uses a "coach intensive" program where most of the screening and recommendation of agents is done by the school's coaching staff. Witte stunned representatives from NCAA member institutions at a career counseling panel forum conducted by the NCAA in November of 1989 by announcing in his keynote address that he had no use for the panels. "Arkansas never had and never will have a screening panel,"[36] Witte told the group at the beginning of his talk. Although he did eventually state after a question and answer period that he would reconsider his position, his initial view was clear: "I think the only realistic way to go is to have the coach involved. Much of what panels are supposed to do I question how competent they are. I think coaches are better suited."[37]

In furtherance of NCAA educational efforts a player/agent educational videotape is being developed.[38] The projected budget for the tape is $20,000. In it respected athletes and officials discuss NCAA rules and the problems with contracting with an agent before one's eligibility expires. Some professional teams also provide player-education programs. The San Francisco 49ers and Golden State Warriors counsel athletes at the professional level. In a program run by Dr. Harry Edwards, a professor of sociology at the University of California at Berkeley, both teams have regular sessions to assist the athletes in matters that relate directly to agents.

Chapter 8

"Shake 'em Hard in the Sports Side": Revision and Enforcement of Existing Laws and Regulations

In a recruiting pitch to an athlete, sports agent Norby Walters said, "The normal sports agent . . . he's not gonna shake white America. I have been shaking those people for years in that music side of entertainment. Now it's time to shake 'em hard in the sports side of entertainment."[1] The "shaking" needs to come from the regulators of the sports-agent industry.

Making use of the laws that already exist is one of the most important keys to the regulation of sports agents. As Chapter 4 illustrates, there are plenty of laws and certification programs that can be used to regulate the sports agent. Senator John Culver maintains that enforcement should remain in the private sector with some degree of government coordination: "I don't think it defies the imagination of man or woman to come up with something that makes sense."[2] This chapter examines some of the problems with the existing regulations. It further examines the need for more rigorous enforcement of existing regulations and looks at the need for a uniform sports agent law.

Three major flaws afflict most existing state athlete/agent statutes: conflict-of-law issues, the commerce clause, and, most importantly, quality assurance. In addition, certain other weaknesses characterize most of the present legislation. These will be discussed below. Where the statutes may be most effective is in aiding in the prosecution of undesired behavior once it occurs. The statutes make some activities, such as violating or causing an athlete to violate an NCAA rule, a civil or maybe even a criminal violation. Where advancing money to a student athlete is not illegal normally, it can be made illegal by this new type of statute.

Problems with Existing Legislation

Conflict of Laws

The first major problem with the existing state regulations is the conflict of laws raised by the national character of college athletics. For example, may California enforce its registration requirements against an Ohio resident who attempts to represent a student athlete from a California school? Should Ohio's regulation govern the activities of this same agent while he or she is in California "recruiting" the client? The law has not yet resolved the answers to these questions. In developing new laws, legislators have tried to remain aware of these jurisdictional problems. An Oklahoma legislator has noted that athlete agents who do not live in Oklahoma "don't pay any attention" to the law.[3]

This problem is particularly hard on the sports agent who is trying to comply with state regulations. Is it necessary to pay the registration fee in one state but not the other? Which state's reporting procedure must the agent comply with?

Commerce Clause

Another problem with existing regulations is whether the commerce clause of the United States Constitution would bar the enforcement of any of these state regulations.[4] The commerce clause bars states from regulating affairs of interstate commerce—that is, issues that affect several states. Railroads and airlines are two common examples of entities that are regulated by the federal government rather than by the individual states. Rather than allowing the states to regulate what types of railroad car coupling must be used and thus run the risk of having to change couplings each time a state border is passed, the federal government establishes guidelines for all interstate commerce.

There is precedent for the successful assertion of the commerce clause in barring state regulation of sports in other affairs. In *City of Oakland v. Oakland Raiders* the city of Oakland, California was barred by the courts from exercising eminent domain rights over a sports franchise because such an action would interfere with interstate commerce.[5] That case was one of several pieces of litigation in the saga of the Raiders NFL franchise in their move from Oakland to Los Angeles. The city of Oakland instituted an action that sought to "condemn" the sports franchise, much in the way municipalities condemn and take homes and other property to construct freeways, parks, or airports. The taking of a sports franchise under this eminent-domain principle was a novel idea, but one that looked like it might prove to be successful. Instead of reaching its decision on the facts of the case—whether this was the type of property a city could condemn and keep in the city for the public interest—the court ruled that the commerce clause barred the city from taking such an action. The court reasoned that the sport is an interstate affair and that only the federal government should be able to regulate those activities.

A similar argument could be made that the regulation of sports agents is not a state but a federal affair. A defense of this nature could be used by a sports agent if a state attempted to prosecute under a state regulation. How successful it would be remains to be seen.

Quality Assurance

Another major component lacking in these statutes, and without a doubt the most important, is a quality-assurance measure. Unlike obtaining a driver's license or a license to practice law or medicine, state regulations contain no testing procedure. Although all the statutes make various queries regarding education and other skill levels, none thus far has established any minimum competency standards. Texas requires employment records and addresses, Oklahoma requires five references, Louisiana requires three references, and Iowa requires the disclosure of any misdemeanor or felony convictions.[6] Becoming a "licensed" agent in most states is the equivalent of walking into a motor vehicles office, announcing that you want to drive, paying a fee, and walking out with a license.

All regulations aimed specifically at sports agents should have a minimum substantive skill-level requirement. Those individuals who desire to register as sports agents and do not have this minimum level should be denied registration or certification. Not only should the players' associations actively deny certification to unqualified individuals, those states which have and are contemplating legislation should actively screen registrants by establishing minimum substantive skill levels. States may come up with some basic educational requirements or some form of straightforward standardized test. Some form of character assessment is needed as well.

The federal legislation proposed by Congressman John Bryant recognizes the need to deal with these two issues, although some of the specifics are still lacking. Setting forth guidelines on quality the legislation states:

No registered sports agent shall effect any transaction in, or induce the formation of, any agent contract or sports contract, unless such sports agent meets standards of capability, and such sports agent and all natural persons associated with such sports agent meet such standards of training, experience, competence, and such other qualifications, as a national sports agency association or the Secretary finds necessary or appropriate in the public interest or for the protection of athletes. A national sports agency association shall establish such standards by rules which may specify that all or any part of such standards shall apply to any class of sports agents and persons associated with such sports agents.

The states should also retain whatever rights they have established for themselves to deny registration for prior criminal, civil, or other unethical activities. If these entities do not establish minimum competency requirements their licensing or certification does more harm than good. A student athlete who has read a long list of licenses and certifications possessed by an agent has been done a tremendous disservice. The student athlete, like most people, will believe that these types of accreditations indicate that the sports agent is qualified. That is clearly not necessarily the case, and the confusion such accreditations can cause is one of the key reasons why the NCAA discontinued its voluntary registration program.

Conflict of Interest and Excessive Fees

Two further areas that any new statute should address are the conflict-of-interest and excessive-fee issues. Attorneys who represent athletes must conform with a canon of ethics that guards against trying to represent the interest of two clients that might conflict without disclosing the conflict to the respective clients. The scenarios in Chapter 2 where agents represent conflicting interests would properly have to be disclosed by attorneys to their clients. Non-attorneys have no similar requirement absent legislation. Although some states are mindful of this, others have neglected to include an appropriate provision.

Another concern about these state regulations is the excessive fees that sports agents may have to pay to comply with registration in a number of states where they may do business. Not only do agents have to pay registration fees in these states but many require them to post a bond as well. If all fifty states had a statute requiring this, the cost of entering the sports agent business could be tens of thousands of dollars. Sports agent Craig Fenech maintains that he cannot find an entity that will provide him with a bond for his business. If his experience is typical, such requirements would effectively restrict the number of people to a select category of the well-financed. Those excluded would undoubtedly include many talented and conscientious individuals; those admitted might be able to raise enough money for fees but might not make as meaningful a contribution. Moreover, the need for thousands of dollars might in itself be a corrupting factor for agents without enough money, who would have to seek financial support from other backers. These "silent partners" might be of questionable integrity.

Vigorous Enforcement of Existing Laws

That non-sports-agent-specific regulations can be used effectively was illustrated by the federal convictions of Norby Walters and Lloyd Bloom, as well as the state prosecutions of the same parties, of agent Jim Abernethy, and, earlier, of Richard Sorkin. Most of the fraud or income mismanagement issues can be attacked by utilizing these laws.

But conviction is not necessarily deterrence. Even after conviction, all charges against agent Norby Walters in Alabama were dropped when he paid the University of Alabama a settlement of $200,000.[7] Similarly, Walters's associate Lloyd Bloom received a sentence that required him to serve one week of a one-year sentence washing state trooper cars while staying at the hotel of his choice.[8] Finally, all charges against agent Jim Abernethy were thrown out at the appellate level.[9] The sentences against Bloom and Walters in their federal trial are probably the greatest deterrents presently in place.

The focus of regulating sports agents should be placed on enforcing these existing laws and not in incorporating outdated concepts of amateurism into new regulations. The focus should be on any illegal activities in recruiting athletes and any violations once an agreement is entered into. These are the types of activities, as with any industry, that public entities should expend their limited resources on, not in seeking to regulate activities where no one is harmed. Many contend that already limited law enforcement resources should not be used to police amateurism. The NCAA appears to have the clearest responsibility in that regard, if amateurism is a goal it chooses to preserve. If the cloak of amateurism is removed, even to a limited degree, then some of the opportunity for agents is removed as well. But any type of payment to athletes, from small stipends to salaries, from endorsements to loans to an open market for payments by agents, has to be made by the NCAA. Law enforcement should focus on the issues addressed in the Sorkin, Abernethy, and Walters and Bloom cases. Individuals with private causes of action must assert their rights as well. For some activities a private civil suit may be the only manner of regulating the activity.

In *U.S. v. Walters-Bloom* the criminal application of the RICO Act was deemed appropriate by the jury. In that case the "pattern of racketeering" was the mail fraud that resulted against the NCAA when the student athletes paid by Walters and Bloom had letters sent to the NCAA by their schools proclaiming that they were eligible to compete under NCAA rules when, in fact, they were not.

That case did have the added involvement of an organized crime figure, Michael Franzese, who allegedly helped finance Walters's and

Bloom's venture into the sports agent business in exchange for a 25 percent share.[10] It does not seem, however, that Franzese's involvement was an essential element in the jury's determination. Thus, as is the case with so many RICO actions to date, the organized-crime component may not need to be present at all; all that apparently needs to occur is for an agent to induce two athletes to violate an NCAA regulation and for those athletes to proclaim to his institution and the NCAA that they are eligible.

Apart from any actual criminal or civil violations that may occur, the government or a private citizen may bring a RICO action as well. Basic standards of prosecutor discretion will probably keep the criminal RICO statute in check and prevent an overabundance of these actions. The civil RICO problems that have confronted brokerage houses and others would probably not be so problematic in the agent business.

Successful legal actions may be brought against student athletes who participate in the fraud as well. Philadelphia Eagles wide receiver Cris Carter was fined $15,000 and ordered to perform 600 hours of community service for failing to cooperate with federal authorities when they were investigating Walters and Bloom. Carter failed to reveal that he had received a $5,000 signing incentive from agent David Lueddeke.[11]

Many commentators have maintained that the best way to remedy agent problems would be with strong federal legislation providing appropriate sanctions. Federal legislation certainly would provide uniformity in addressing the industry, eliminating the conflict-of-law and commerce-clause problems. However, federal legislation in the sports-agent field will probably continue to be met with little success. Lloyd Shefsky, former president of the Sports Lawyers Association and a veteran of a three year lobbying effort for sports-agent legislation, cites three reasons for the lack of success in getting a measure passed: "The first was it was not as important as current events like the arms race; second, the former jocks like [New Jersey Senator Bill] Bradley and [New York Representative Jack] Kemp did not want to be associated with sports; and third, and this is the best of all, they said, 'You want us to protect millionaires?'"[12] Even if such legislation were passed, there is clear evidence that in other professions where legislation exists to control the professional ethics—securities brokers as a notable example—fraud and unethical activities may continue to permeate the industry. Ivan Boesky and Michael Milken were both aware of the rules against insider trading, but because of the potential for huge profits, they took the risk of breaking the laws and getting caught.[13]

Uniform Laws

What is not in place that may prove useful is a Uniform Agent Regulation Law. If no federal legislation is forthcoming, an alternative would be to have the laws in each of the states be identical. The drafting of a uniform law or a model act certainly would not be unique.[14] The most obvious examples are the existence of the Model Penal Code and the Uniform Commercial Code. The following synopsis explains the process by which a proposed subject develops into a uniform law.[15]

Uniform laws are promulgated by the National Conference of Commissioners on Uniform State Laws.[16] This organization consists of commissioners appointed by the governors of the fifty states, the District of Columbia, and Puerto Rico. The process by which commissioners are appointed can differ depending on the state,[17] but all commissioners are members of the bar. The conference meets annually, immediately preceding the American Bar Association annual meeting.[18]

The National Conference is composed of a standing and a special committee. The standing committee investigates the appropriateness of various subjects recommended to the conference as the basis for a uniform act. Upon approval of a subject by the conference, a special committee of commissioners is appointed to prepare drafts of the act. The conference votes whether to promulgate the uniform act only after the proposed acts are reviewed, line by line, by the entire body. In addition, the acts must be considered during at least two annual meetings.[19]

Once a uniform act is passed by the conference and endorsed by the American Bar Association, its enactment is urged in each state. When the conference finds that uniformity is desirable but not necessary, a uniform law will be promulgated as a model act.

A uniform law or model act would be the one place that all the key parties concerned with the agent-regulation problem could come together to develop a law that would be in the best interest of all concerned parties. Any uniform law would have to resolve the problem of paying a licensing fee or posting a bond in several states as well as resolving jurisdiction issues. Presumably the law could specify where the agent must be registered. That would prevent an agent's having to pay a fee in more than one state unless operating an office in more than one state. States can assert jurisdiction under these statutes to prosecute agents to the fullest extent allowed by the Constitution. Thus, a state's ability to use its statute against an agent licensed in another state would be permitted to the degree allowed by the latest U.S. Supreme Court pronouncement regarding "long arm" jurisdiction.

That such a code might work is attested to by the success of the Uniform Commercial Code. The Uniform Commercial Code is discussed by James White and Robert Summers as though it was one of the most spectacular success stories in American law.[20] A primary reason for its development was the need for uniformity in the law of business dealings. Today forty-nine of the fifty states have adopted one of three different official texts of the Uniform Commercial Code, Louisiana being the only state that has not. This has occurred without a congressional action, although there have been calls by scholars for a "federal" uniform commercial code.

The UCC was developed by the National Conference of Commissioners on Uniform State Laws and the American Law Institute. The activity to reform the existing commercial laws and other uniform acts in existence began in the 1930s and 1940s. Although there were uniform acts in existence regarding a variety of commercial subjects, not all states enacted them as law. Therefore, the goal of uniformity regarding commercial transactions was not taking place.

The present accomplishment of forty-nine states' having virtually the same laws for commercial transactions was achieved by bringing together all the interested parties and their diverse interests to develop a draft of the Uniform Commercial Code. Although actual work began on the code in 1944, the first state to adopt the uniform model was Pennsylvania in 1953 and not until 1968 was the UCC adopted by forty-nine states. In 1974 even Louisiana adopted a few of its sections.

The Uniform Commercial Code is a complex document of nearly one thousand pages. A uniform agent statute would not require that sort of detail. Because of its relative simplicity, it would not take as long for the drafters to develop a model act. Once this uniform law is in place and assuming it drops outdated concepts of amateurism, the rules of the agent business will be more clearly defined. If requirements are added, the unqualified agents can be weeded out.

Who should be involved in the drafting? Clearly there should be individuals to represent the interests of all the parties that have attempted to promulgate some sort of regulations. These parties would include state representatives, unions, the NCAA, agents, athletes, and others.

A uniform law does not bar the application of existing laws to violations that may occur. For example, the Uniform Commercial Code specifically states in Section 1-103:

Unless displaced by the particular provisions of this Act, the principles of law and equity . . . shall supplement its provisions.

This means that existing laws for fraud, embezzlement, or whatever else remain applicable. Further, if a federal act is ever passed by Congress it displaces the uniform law, as it would become the uniform law of the land.

Again, it must be acknowledged that a uniform federal law would be the ideal foundation for the problems in the industry. This is so not just because of the statement that it would make but also because uniform laws are not necessarily uniform. As was noted initially, various versions of the Uniform Commercial Code have been adopted. Even within the states that have adopted the same versions many states have made revisions appropriate for their own jurisdictions. This could not be done with a federal statute.

Absent a federal law, however, a uniform sports-agent law would not be a total solution, but it would at least bring together the regulatory ideas of the key parties and present a vehicle for uniformity. The uniform commission could develop, for example, a model statute incorporating the best from the existing state statutes. The commission would be wise to insert minimum qualifications or provisions for testing. Similarly, the statute should make provisions for reciprocity with other states that adopt the model statute. If this does come about, then there is a possibility of referring to the regulation issues in this industry as a success story approaching the spectacular description that White and Summers gave of the Uniform Commercial Code.

Senator John Culver is a strong supporter of a presidential commission to study the problem with one possible recommendation being the development of a uniform law. Culver was a member of the presidential commission that studied Olympic sports in 1970. The federal law governing amateur sports was developed out of that commission. Similarly, Craig Fenech, the chairman of the Sports Lawyers Association committee on federal regulation of sports agents, would like to see "one set of regulations or alternatively one per sport."[21] Reggie Wilkes expresses a similar view regarding the need for the sometimes diverging organizations to agree: "The various organizations should come together as one. They've got to come to some common ground."[22]

Players' Association Certification and Decertification

Even with a uniform law in place the players' unions will continue to play a prominent role in agent regulation. Now that players' associations have asserted their right to certify agents with a degree of success, they should act more assertively to deny initial certification to incompetent and dishonest agents and to "decertify" agents who become involved in improprieties. The NBPA has taken a step in this direction and decertified one agent for making payments to college, junior college, and high school coaches who helped him obtain clients.[23] An NFL agent was decertified for mishandling of funds.[24] The players' associations should take strong public stances against other agents who commit some of the wrongs discussed. Decertification is a vehicle that may accomplish this goal. The unions should also clearly assert their authority over the sports agent/student athlete relationship.

The influence of the agent on the career and financial health of an athlete makes it crucial that the athletes understand what decertification means. When one athlete was informed his agent had been decertified, he said, "I'm still not quite clear on why he can't negotiate my contracts."[25]

NBPA Executive Director Charles Grantham indicates that the NBPA will be moving toward a more rigid certification program, one requiring a thoroughly qualitative investigation and disclosure before licensing is granted. He further indicates that a formal random financial audit system may be put in place. Under this system any certified agent could be subject to an audit by a major accounting firm selected by the union.

In 1987 it was reported that 750 agents were registered with the NFLPA, which only had 1,260 members at that time. Similarly the NBA in 1987 had 276 players and 208 registered agents.[26] Clearly there is no shortage of sports agents and tighter scrutiny at the certification stage certainly seems appropriate.

The number of agents in both leagues has decreased as the fee for certification has increased. In 1989 the NFLPA fee was $400 and the NBPA fee $800. A more aggressive certification and screening process by the players associations adds strength and could increase the accountability of the agents to the unions that have granted them the authority to negotiate contracts.[27] One additional possibility is that the unions establish a uniform certification program for all sports. At a minimum the unions could benefit by exchanging information on improprieties by any of their certified agents.

One concern, however, in aggressively screening agents on the front end is an antitrust action by an excluded agent. Such an action might be barred by the labor exemption to the antitrust laws.[28]

Doug Allen of the NFLPA maintains that the union would like to move aggressively to pursue agents who have violated the union guidelines: "When we get evidence we take action. The biggest problem is the unwillingness of players' agents to provide us with evidence. When we get in front of an arbitrator we have to be able to prove it." Allen emphasized to a meeting of sports agents, "If you've got evidence, we want it. If you are willing to testify, we'll take it."

In 1990 the NFLPA decertified itself as the official bargaining unit of the NFL players. The union took this step to attempt to resolve an ongoing dispute with NFL management. As a result, the NFLPA certification program was suspended and a voluntary program took its place. It remains to be seen what changes this may cause, but it is likely that the voluntary program will not cause things to get better.

The MLBPA has begun to become more actively involved in athlete/agent financial disputes as well. Under their arbitration procedures agent Peter Huthwaite sought to recover $28,000 in what he claimed were back fees from the Minnesota Twins' Wally Beckman.[29]

If some of these positive steps are taken the sports-agent industry will provide an improved quality of service across the board. Without reforms, headlines of athletes being harmed by sports agents will continue to appear in the nation's press.

Chapter 9

The Future of the Business

What this book has attempted to present, in addition to an overview of the current state of the law, are some reforms that the relevant parties might make in regulating sports agents. As state legislatures continue to formulate laws in this area, it is important that they assess what it is they want the law to accomplish and why. Their focus should be on screening those who enter the field rather than catching those who violate NCAA rules, unless NCAA rules are reformed to take into account the reformed status of the amateur athlete. All members of the NCAA should bear in mind what Lord Killanin said when he was elected president of the International Olympic Committee: "I do not believe in professional Olympics; I do not believe in open Olympics; but I think we have to realize that we are about to enter the last quarter of the Twentieth Century."[1] Collegiate sports are now entering the twenty-first century and the collegiate version of amateurism must be reformed.

The sports-agent business itself can head in only one of two directions. First, the competition for clients can continue to grow as the salaries of the athletes increase. This is the most likely direction. This course cries out for the reforms proposed. The other possibility is the incorporation of a fixed-wage scale in professional sports. A fixed-wage scale for many reasons is problematic and not one of the remedies suggested here, but it would eliminate the need for agents to negotiate player salaries. This course is unlikely, although occasionally raised by players' unions, because it would probably deprive the superstar athletes of their supersalaries. Even if a fixed-wage scale developed, sports agents would still be around to negotiate endorsement contracts, and the competition for those would probably become more intense.

Since agents are going to remain with us, reforms have to be incorporated to remove the corruption from the industry. Some of the reforms suggested here remove the opportunity that currently presents itself to the dishonest and incompetent sports agent. The reforms should also lead to an increased level of information about agents among the NCAA, its member institutions, the leagues, and the players' unions. This should help to reduce these problems as well. Other unscrupulous activities should continue to be prosecuted under the laws of the individual states and the federal government.

The NCAA may have to be the most active entity in making these reforms. In the early 1990s, starting with the annual convention, the NCAA did begin to take steps that showed that it recognized the need for change.

At this time, the professional sports leagues are probably the least active entity in the regulating of sports agents. They should at least utilize their financial resources for educational purposes. By becoming involved in education and by establishing a loan program, they can begin to play a more affirmative role. The pro leagues are not without guilt in "corrupting" amateurs. In 1959, general manager of the Los Angeles Rams Pete Rozelle signed collegiate All-American Billy Cannon to a professional contract before the completion of his collegiate career.[2] Other big-name athletes of the day signed early as well. Here the reason for cheating, even by the future commissioner of the NFL, was the competition for talent between the NFL and the then rival American Football League.

University leaders as well have historically been involved in these activities that are contrary to the amateur tradition. For example, in 1902 Henry P. Wright, Dean of the Yale College faculty, wrote the following letter to Yale's legendary football coach Walter Camp regarding an athlete named Cornelius Daly:

Dear Mr. Camp,

Has anything been done for Daly? I understand that some grad could be found from whom he might borrow $100 occasionally, giving his note, to be paid after graduation. He is pretty hard up and is getting rather restless. I do not see how he can come back after this term unless he is able to raise something somewhere.[3]

The obvious implication is that this Ivy League institution had a method in place for under-the-table payments. The idea of competing for the best athletes is not one that the agents, the NCAA, or the unions alone should have to sort out.

It is important to recognize that providing student athletes with a student life stipend, allowing them to work, and allowing them to endorse products would go strongly against long-standing definitions of amateurism. The NFL faced a similar dilemma regarding the drafting of underclassmen. State regulations that require agent registration and do not address competency are clearly not enough. Obviously an attempt to put *all* the reforms discussed in place is not practical or feasible. However, at least a serious review of the reforms is necessary for the positive impact they can have in decreasing the negative impact a sports agent can have on a young athlete's life. The key parties in this industry, however, are beginning to work more closely together. That communication between the diverse entities involved is the overall key. From the empirical experience over the past several years it is evident that no entity acting alone can resolve the problems of the industry. Communication between sectors is the initial step. Once that communication is in place, constructive change is almost certain.

Federal legislation, such as that proposed by Senator Bryant, would have a positive impact if it were enforced vigorously. If that cannot be done, and history indicates that it cannot, the second best solution is a set of uniform laws developed by a uniform law commission much like the Uniform Commercial Code. With this in place, each state could adopt the code and provide reciprocity to agents who successfully register in another state.

A new federal or uniform law alone will not be enough. In other businesses where laws have long been in place, people still cheat when they see a financial advantage in doing so. The reality must be faced that some people will always cheat where there is a cash benefit. Thirty-four of the forty-five schools placed on probation by the NCAA in 1988 were penalized because of improper payments to student athletes.[4] What is needed is to reduce the possibility of cheating and preventing those that cheat from cheating again. To reduce cheating some type of increased income for student athletes is essential. Increasing the stipend that student athletes receive seems to be the most palatable idea. Roger Noll suggests that, much like the "salary cap" used by the NBA, the member institutions be given a set amount that they may use to pay student athletes. Noll writes, as an example, that each school could be allowed to spend $250,000 beyond what it spends on scholarships, with an additional cap of $25,000 allowable to each student athlete. The precise allocation, according to Noll, would be up to the individual schools: season-ending awards, straight salaries, and signing bonuses are three examples suggested.[5]

Paying athletes at this level should not offend American sensibilities in the manner that it supposedly does. The Greek model of athletics apparently allowed athletes to receive compensation. There is economic as well as sociological logic to paying student athletes some level of increased compensation.

In other amateur sports organizations it may continue to make sense not to provide athletes with compensation. In 1989 officials of Little League baseball had to take action to stop incentive payments that were being made to children in a league in that organization. Even nominal payments in that system seem illogical, and have nothing to do with arguments for payments at the NCAA level. There is no reason to fear that pay at the collegiate level will inspire a trend.[6]

Athletes must be able to receive more income as students. The logical entities to provide these increased funds are, first, the member institutions and, if that is not financially feasible, then the NCAA. At a minimum the additional amount the student athlete receives should be equal to an amount that brings the spending money available to the student athlete up to that available to the university's average student. This amount may be enough to prevent substantial cheating. If not, the amount should be increased.

The idea of establishing a separate minor league system with home teams centered on campuses seems wholly unattractive. Although it leaves a cleaner taste in the mouths of those who are against the payments to amateurs, it removes an incentive from many of our youth to attend college. While it is true that some athletes only attend college to participate in sports anyway, the NCAA is striving against that motivation by measures such as Propositions 42 and 48, which set forth minimum educational requirements for student athletes.

Allowing athletes to receive endorsement income appears to be more problematic, not because the athletes would be receiving income, but because the sports agent may begin to play an integral role in the athletes' career at a stage that would, again, encourage cheating. It is difficult to imagine a system that would allow an athlete to work with an agent in a financial transaction as a freshman or sophomore without the agent's beginning to utilize the tactics that have been prevalent near the end of the student athlete's career. As Pam Lester notes, this could open up a whole new set of problems.

But if the receipt of cash for endorsements is not a problem in itself, should student athletes be able to negotiate endorsement contracts on their own? Can an athlete endorse a local automobile dealership if the owner is a booster or alumnus? What happens if the amount received is disproportionate to what is generally perceived as reasonable for such an endorsement? A solution that has some merit is allowing the endorsement of specific products, such as athletic shoes. These companies would not have an independent incentive, as a booster does, to pay more than the athlete's actual market value. Such endorsements would allow the athlete to receive additional revenues from a natural market source. They would also deal with the fairness issue of coaches receiving all the shoe endorsement income.

A last resort for the income problems are loans. For these, again, the individual member institutions and the NCAA are the logical source. Although the institutions and the NCAA are not in the banking business, the investment may prove in the long run to be advantageous. A loan may keep the student athlete in the college ranks longer. In addition to removing the incentive to take money from an agent, the loan provides an incentive for the athlete to stay in school.

Much like a bank, the NCAA can make loans based on information received from NCAA or professional scouting sources. Further, if the professional leagues cooperate, the loan agreement can require automatic repayment to be made to the NCAA from the salary earned by the professional team the athlete eventually plays for. Loans from the league itself are not as attractive as those from the NCAA because the teams really do not have the same incentive to make the loans that the NCAA does. The ultimate stop for the athlete is the professional league, which may not really care whether the athlete stays in school. Either loan program is viable but the NCAA program, particularly given its current prosperity and its desired continued prosperity, seems to be most appropriate. Alternatively, either the NCAA or the pro leagues may be able to develop a relationship with banking institutions that will make loans based on a professional athletic potential.

Once some of the monetary incentive to cheat has been removed, another major need is to ensure that only quality agents are allowed to practice the trade. Just as with any other profession, if agents are not qualified, they should not be allowed to practice. If they do something wrong, their right to practice should be taken away. If the states stay involved in the process, or if a uniform law or federal law is adopted, minimum standards must be established and maintained. A prospective agent who does not meet the standards cannot be an agent; to fall below the standards is to lose the right.

The NCAA does not have the resources to police agent standards and in this one aspect has wisely dropped out of the certification business. Their rule should remain strongest in the area of education and in ensuring, as with any other student, that the student athlete makes the wisest decision possible regarding his professional career. The fledgling career-counseling panels may be the best avenue for this.

Edward King feels that if the NCAA does stay involved in policing agents it should use the resources available to it more fully: "The territory is not that big. A personal computer at each member institution loaded with information about agents could work wonders." King envisions a system in which the players' associations and the states would give general information about agents, as well as information about agent lawsuits and other actions, to the NCAA. This could then be distributed on a database along with the names of other athletes the agent has represented. King says such an "information depot" "could fill a tremendous void in the amount of information the student athlete receives." He also says that "the NCAA could mandate that any student athlete who has the opportunity to become a professional must review this available information."[7] Southern Methodist University now requires that all student athletes take a course on NCAA rules and also discuss career-counseling issues. SMU has suffered severely by violating NCAA rules in the past; so the fact that it requires such a class is not surprising. Other institutions may find it wise to follow its lead on a preventative measure.

The certification and decertification obligations should fall most strongly on the professional league player associations. Management within these leagues must cooperate in not negotiating with an agent unless that agent is certified.

Even with these changes in place, the problems typified by Walters and Bloom will continue to occur to some degree. Where such incidents do occur, or where other laws are broken, the applicable laws must be vigorously enforced. The continual application of RICO should have a chilling effect on potential wrongdoers. The U.S. district attorney in the Walters-Bloom trial expressed concern over the influence organized crime could have over collegiate and professional sports if rules violations such as payments to athletes continue. He cites the fact that Michael Franzese, a member of the Columbo crime family, was a financier of the Walters-Bloom firm, World Sports & Entertainment. Regarding this financing Franzese told *Sports Illustrated* reporter Bruce Selcraig, "Look, we were business associates. I'm not going to lie and say we weren't. But to say I had anything to do with his sports business, that I controlled it or called the shots, is ridiculous."[8] The district attorney, Anton Valukas, feared that an organized crime connection of this nature could place pressure on players to shave points or otherwise throw sporting events to serve the purposes of their underworld benefactors.[9] In March of 1990 former North Carolina State University star Charles Shackleford was accused of being in a similar sort of point-shaving arrangement. In an emotional press conference, Shackleford denied that any point shaving had taken place in connection with $65,000 he had received from two men when he was a sophomore and a junior. Part of the money, which Shackleford characterized as a loan he repaid, was paid by Larry Gillman, called a "coach-turned-agent" by the *New York Times,* who hoped to represent Shackleford in his negotiations with the NBA. Shackleford ultimately selected another agent.[10]

If a member of organized crime is financing the payments the agent is making to the athlete, in some way that athlete is indebted to organized crime. According to investigative author Dan Moldea, Walters and Franzese allegedly used similar aggressive practices in attempting to become involved in the Jacksons' Victory Tour in 1984. The Victory Tour was one of the largest tours of all time by a singing group and, not unexpectedly, a number of individuals wanted to reap some of the financial benefits. Moldea writes:

> Franzese later testified that he had tried to muscle the Jacksons' manager Ronald Weisner. "We decided that Norby would make it known who I was and who I was associated with . . . and I would do my best to convince them that they should do the tour with Norby."
> "I explained to him [Weisner] that if Norby wasn't involved in the tour in some manner there wasn't going to be a tour."[11]

There have certainly been enough scandals in professional and amateur sports for the next step to be understood. The potential for this corruption makes the rationale for eliminating the student athlete's need for additional funds or bringing the payments above the table all the more clear. Ideally, the payments should be eliminated altogether by using the methods discussed. If this cannot be done, then making the incentive signing bonuses aboveboard would eliminate the possibility of using the threat of disclosure to influence the play of the athlete.

The globalization of sports, with the development of international sports leagues, is making the sports-agent business an international business. It is difficult enough to regulate the activities of domestic agents. What happens when agents who are citizens of Japan or Italy begin to negotiate contracts for American athletes? Sports agents have begun to play a more active role not only in finding employment for athletes in foreign leagues, particularly in basketball and hockey. In 1989, agents began to play a role in helping Soviet citizens defect in order to play in the NHL; agent Rich Winter is acquiring a reputation for having helped a number of hockey stars defect from behind the Iron Curtain.

The future of the sports-agent industry, and particularly its regulation, is closely tied to reforms that take place in college sports in general. The problems in college sports go way beyond sports agents.[12] The reality that sports have become more than extracurricular activity must be accepted. With the elevation of sports to this higher level a reevaluation of all the surrounding circumstances must be made, not just in terms of sports agents but in terms of college sports in general and the level of education that the students are receiving. An increased level of so-called "professionalism" in college sports should not be feared. It may be the transition itself that is the most difficult step to take. For a long time the tennis world regarded professional athletes as manual laborers. It took "Cash and Carry" Pyle to help change that perception. When he finally convinced the female sensation of the day, Suzanne Lenglen, to accept his offer to turn professional the press acknowledged that she "was not denigrating herself but uplifting the world of sport."[13]

There are much broader issues, not addressed here, that any attempt at reforming college sports must examine. The threshold questions were raised in the preface of the Carnegie Report in 1929:

"What relation has this astonishing athletic display to the work of an intellectual agency like a university?"

"How do students, devoted to study, find either the time or the money to stage so costly a performance?"[14]

Whoever can answer and justify their answers to these questions raised over sixty years ago can go a long way in resolving not only the sports-agent problem but the other problems in college sports today.

Senator Culver's call for a presidential commission to examine sports agents is a wise one. There should also be a specific commission to examine what is happening with the education of our student athletes. If these steps are not taken, much of what happens in the future may be controlled by the courts. In sentencing Walters and Bloom—Walters to five years in prison and Bloom to three years in prison and three years probation—United States District Court Judge George M. Marovich said:

If Mr. Walters and Mr. Bloom are guilty, so too may be many alumni, boosters and coaches. I want to give fair warning to people who violate the rules. You may be playing in a different ballgame now, and it may be hardball. There's a new player on the field—the rule of law.[15]

Even if affirmative steps are taken, collegiate athletics may never return to a time of raccoon coats, tailgate parties, and fight songs. But some action will remove the constant association of college sports with the scandalous headlines of the 1980s. Collegiate athletics must now be recognized as big, profit-making entertainment, and reforms must be made that recognize the changing nature of the enterprise.

Appendixes

Appendix I: Association of Representatives of Professional Athletes (ARPA) Code of Ethics

Canon One

"A Representative shall maintain the highest degree of integrity and competence in representing the professional athlete."

Rule 1-101 Representing Clients with Competence & Integrity

(A) A Representative shall not:
  (1) Violate a rule of conduct of this Code,
  (2) Use another to circumvent a rule of this Code,
  (3) Engage in illegal conduct involving a felony or conduct involving moral turpitude,
  (4) Engage in conduct involving dishonesty, fraud, deceit, or misinterpretation,
  (5) Engage in conduct prejudicial to the reasonable conduct of professional athletics,
  (6) Engage in conduct which adversely reflects on his fitness.

Rule 1-102 Information Regarding a Violation of this Code

(A) A Representative possessing information which is unprivileged as a matter of law and not protected by Rule 4-101 of this Code concerning a violation of Rule 1-101 shall report such information to the Committee on Discipline of the Association of Representatives of Professional Athletes immediately.
(B) A Representative shall be available to testify or produce a statement under oath as to the nature, source and details of the information described in Rule 1-102(A).

Rule 1-103 Refusing to Accept a Client

(A) A Representative shall refrain from accepting the representation of a professional athlete when
 (1) The Representative does not possess the competence through training by education or experience in a particular area,
 (2) The Representative's representation of the athlete will create differing or unresolvable conflict of interest with an existing client or with an existing financial enterprise,
 (3) The Representative has differing interests with those of his prospective client.
(B) A Representative must disclose in writing in advance of his representation of a professional athlete the nature and degree of his involvement in any matter in which he is recommending, suggesting, or advising that the athlete invest.

Rule 1-104 General

(A) A Representative shall not knowingly give aid to or cooperate in any way with another in conduct which would violate this Code.
(B) A Representative shall act in the best interests of the professional athlete, bearing in mind the high degree of trust and responsibility reposed in him as fiduciary.
(C) A Representative shall become familiar with the Collective Bargaining Agreement, Standard of Uniform Players Contract, Constitution, Bylaws and League Rules or the League and such other relevant documents affecting wages, hours and working conditions of the players in the sport or sports in which he represents professional athletes.

Canon Two

"A Representative shall be dignified in the conduct of his profession."

Rule 2-101 Representative's Letterhead, Stationery. etc.

(A) A Representative shall not compensate or give anything of value to representatives of the print, video or audio media or other communication media in return for professional publicity.
(B) The professional letterhead, business or calling card, stationery, announcements, office signs of a representative and his firm or organization shall be dignified and may:
 (1) list the representative's name, firm or organization name, firm members and their position,
 (2) list the address of the firm's office or offices, phone number,

telex and other such information as may aid the professional athlete in locating the representative,

(3) indicate his membership in ARPA.

(C) A Representative in the operation of his firm may practice under a trade name, partnership corporation or professional association.

(D) The letterhead of the representative shall indicate the name or names of representatives associated with the firm. If the degree of participation by a representative in the firm is less than that of a partner or manager, the nature of such association shall be indicated on the firm's stationery.

Rule 2-102 A Representative engaged in more than one profession or business

(A) A Representative who is engaged both in representation of professional athletes and simultaneously in another profession or business shall clearly distinguish those businesses or professions on his letterhead, office sign, professional card and other public communication.

(B) A Representative who in addition to his traditional role as a representative, offers to provide services as an investment and/or financial advisor, counselor or director to a professional athlete or in any way assert or maintain control and/or management of the financial affairs of a professional athlete, whether for compensation or not, must be qualified to do so based upon training or experience.

(C) A Representative who assumes the role outlined in Section B of this Rule, shall fully disclose that role in his contract with the professional athlete he represents. Such contract shall provide at least a statement of the services to be provided in connection with investment counseling, the limitations of such services, if any, and the fees to be charged for such services.

(D) A Representative may use or permit the use of, in connection with his name, any earned degree or title.

Rule 2-103 Recommending Employment of the Representative

(A) A Representative shall not compensate in any way or give anything of value or promise to compensate a professional or amateur athlete to recommend or secure the representative's employment in any capacity.

(B) A Representative shall not compensate or give anything of value to any individual as a reward for recommending the representative's employment or for referring an athlete to the representative; except that a representative may pay the customary costs and charges in connection with a Professional Association and with ARPA.

(C) A Representative may receive without the payment of compensation, other than dues, referrals from appropriate referring agencies.

(D) A Representative may employ for compensation, with the consent of his client another representative or other professional to assist him in fulfilling his duties and obligations to a professional athlete he represents.

Rule 2-104 Fees for Service

(A) A Representative shall disclose, in advance of any representation agreement and in writing, the nature of his fees and the services to be performed for the fee.

(B) A Representative shall not enter into an agreement for, charge, or collect an illegal or clearly excessive fee.

(C) A fee is clearly excessive when, after a review of the facts, an individual within the industry of reasonable prudence would be left with the firm conviction that the fee is in excess of a reasonable fee for the work performed.

(D) Among the factors relevant in determining whether a fee is reasonable are:
(1) The time, labor, expenses involved;
(2) The degree of expertise required and the level of expertise of the representative;
(3) The usual and customary charge in the industry for the services performed,
(4) The impact of the services to be performed on the workload of the representative;
(5) The relationship between the fee and the length of the athlete's contract.

(E) In determining his fee, the Representative shall consider the relationship between the fee and foreseeable length of the athlete's employment with the athletic team and shall make every reasonable effort not to inflict serious hardship on the athlete.

(F) A Representative may employ one of the following methods in establishing his fee:
(1) Fixed fee
(2) Percentage fee
(3) Contingent fee

(G) A Representative shall never solicit nor accept any compensation for services rendered in connection with the negotiation of a player contract or in connection with any other services to a professional athlete from a professional athletic team, club or club representative either directly or indirectly.

(1) Prior disclosure of such compensation shall not result in a waiver of the prohibition set forth in 2-104(G).

(2) The prohibition set forth in 2-104(G) may not be waived by prior agreement or by subsequent contract.

Rule 2-105 Financial Payments

(A) A Representative shall not offer, promise or provide financial payments, support or consideration of any kind to an amateur athlete, his family members, athletic coach, director, school official or school with the intent to influence those persons or organizations into recommending that representative for employment by a professional athlete.

(B) The provisions contained in 2-105(A) may not be waived in advance or by subsequent conduct.

Canon Three

"A Representative shall maintain management responsibility for his firm."

Rule 3-101 A Representative working with a non-Representative

(A) A Representative shall not share fees with a non-Representative except:

(1) A Representative may, with the prior consent of the professional athlete he represents, retain the services of another professional or business entity on behalf of the athlete.

(2) All charges in connection with such work shall be billed to the athlete directly or, at least, must be separately listed on the representative's bill for services.

Rule 3-102 A Representative and the Player Contract

(A) A Representative shall not negotiate or agree to, on behalf of an athlete, any provision in a player contract which directly or indirectly violates or circumvents an operative collective bargaining agreement.

(B) All Representatives shall have a written contract with their clients which fully discloses all fees, duties and responsibilities. Such contract shall fully disclose all matters in which the representative will receive a financial benefit.

(C) Any dispute arising out of a matter other than a dispute over fee shall be resolved by binding arbitration before an impartial arbitration panel set up for the particular sport in accordance with the rules of the American Arbitration Association.

(D) The supervision and administration of the binding arbitration shall be conducted by ARPA.

Canon Four

"A Representative shall preserve the confidence of his client."

Rule 4-101 Maintaining the confidences of the client

(A) A Representative shall not knowingly reveal information of any sort given to him by a client in the course of their professional relationship and which the client reasonably expects to be kept confidential.
(B) A Representative shall not use such confidential information to the direct or indirect disadvantage, harm, or damage of the client.
(C) A Representative shall not use such confidential information for his own advantage unless the client consents in advance after full disclosure by the representative.

Rule 4-102 Confidential information defined

(A) Confidential information refers to information gained in the course of the professional relationship between a representative and a professional athlete which the athlete has requested to be held confidential or which the representative knows or should know would be embarrassing or detrimental to the athlete if released.

Rule 4-103 Representative's Employees

(A) A Representative may reveal:
   (1) Confidential information with the written consent of the client after full disclosure by the representative.
   (2) Confidential information when required by law or directed by a tribunal.
   (3) Confidential information concerning illegal conduct past, present or future on the part of the athlete, except where such information is protected by the attorney/client privilege.

Appendix II: Summary of Selected State Athletic Agent Regulatory Statutes

Alabama

The Alabama Athlete Agency Regulatory Commission is the administrative agency governing sports agents in Alabama. The statute (*Ala. Code* §§8-26-1–41) is applicable to all persons engaged in athlete representation. Any member of the State Bar of Alabama or any other jurisdiction involved in advising an athlete or negotiating an athlete's sports contract is also subject to all the provisions of the statute.

Potential sports agents are required to submit a written application listing their experience in contract negotiations and complaint resolutions. The commission reserves the right to evaluate and investigate the accuracy of the information on the application in determining the eligibility of the sports agent. Once granted, the sports agent's registration is valid for one year. Sports agents are required to pay a filing fee and an annual registration fee to be determined by the commission. They are also required to post a $50,000 surety bond, although the statute does not limit the liability for damages to the amount of the surety bond.

Player/agent contract forms must be approved by the commission and contain an agreement that contractual controversies between the parties must be referred to the commission for adjustment. Sports agents are required to file a schedule of fees, which are limited to 10 percent of the athlete's annual income. Sports agents must keep detailed records of all financial transactions performed on behalf of the athlete.

Violation of the statute constitutes a felony. Penalties include a fine of not more than $5,000 or imprisonment of not less than one year and not more than ten, or both.

California

California is the state that initiated agent regulation, and the administrative agency governing sports agents is the California Labor Commission. Its statute (*Cal. Lab. Code* §§1500–1547) is applicable to any person engaged in athlete representation. However, any member of the State of California Bar, when acting as legal counsel, is exempt from the provisions of the statute.

Potential sports agents are required to submit a written application listing their experience in contract negotiations and complaint resolutions. The commission reserves the right to evaluate and investigate the accuracy of the information on the application in determining the eligibility of the sports agent. Sports agents are required to pay an application fee of $100, an annual fee, and a branch fee the amounts of which are set by the Labor Commissioner in the amount necessary. Once granted, the sports agent's registration is valid for one year. The sports agents are also required to post a $25,000 surety bond, although the statute does not limit the liability for damages to the amount of the surety bond.

Player/agent contract forms must be approved by the Labor Commissioner and contain an agreement that contractual controversies between the parties must be referred to the commission for adjustment. Sports agents are required to file a schedule of fees, which are limited to 10 percent of the athlete's annual income. Sports agents must keep detailed records containing all financial transactions performed on behalf of the athlete.

Sports agents who violate the statute are guilty of a misdemeanor. Penalties include a fine of not less than $500 nor more than $5,000 or imprisonment, or both, for transferring the sports agent's interest without the approval of the Labor Commissioner. For all other violations, the punishment is a fine of not less than $1,000 or imprisonment for not more than ninety days, or both. Unregistered sports agents are prohibited from suing clients for non-payment of fees.

Florida

The Florida Department of Professional Regulation is the administrative agency governing sports agents in Florida. Protecting student athletes and academic institutions was the legislative motivation for creating this statute. For this reason, the statute (*Fla. Stat.* §§468.451–

457) focuses on the regulation of sports agents representing student athletes at colleges or universities in Florida.

Potential sports agents face a felony conviction for failure to register biennially or to pay the $500 registration fee. Surety bonds are not required, and there are no limitations on the fees sports agents may charge.

Sports agents intending to sign a player/agent contract must notify the student athlete's institution. This notification must be made prior to the student athlete's next practice or game, or within seventy-two hours of the signing of the contract, whichever comes first. Sports agents that fail to provide this notification are subject to three sanctions. First, the athlete's agent is guilty of a third-degree felony. Second, the player/agent contract will be declared void and unenforceable. Lastly, the jilted college or university may bring a civil lawsuit against the athlete or sports agent, in which damages may be assessed in an amount equal to three times the value of the student athlete's scholarship.

Georgia

The Georgia Athlete Agent Regulatory Commission is the administrative agency governing sports agents in Georgia. The statute (*Ga. Code Ann.* §§43-4A-1–18) applies to agents representing athletes eligible to participate in intercollegiate sports, as well as previous participants who have never signed a professional sports contract.

Potential sports agents are required to submit a written application listing their experience in contract negotiations and complaint resolutions. The commission reserves the right to evaluate and investigate the accuracy of the information provided on the application in determining the eligibility of the sports agent. The commission may charge an application fee and a temporary registration fee, a registration fee, and a renewal fee. Agents must post a $10,000 surety bond. There are no limitations on the fees sports agents may charge. The content of player/agent contracts need not be given approval, but sports agents must notify the commission of their intent to sign a student athlete to a player/agent contract thirty days prior to the signing of the contract and within 10 days of signing the agent must notify the commission. Otherwise the contract is void. A sports agent who commits violations is guilty of a felony and shall be punished by a fine of not less than $5000 nor more than $100,000 or imprisonment from one to five years, or both. Moreover, the player/agent contract is void if the agent failed to register.

Sports agents who violate the statute may be sued by the aggrieved college or university for damages. However, Georgia is the only state that limits the liability of sports agents to the value of the posted surety bond.

Indiana

The Indiana Agent Licensing Board is the administrative agency governing sports agents in Indiana. The statute (*Ind. Code Ann.* §§35-46-4-1–4) explicitly applies to sports agents representing athletes who are enrolled in college or university and who are eligible to participate in intercollegiate sports.

Sports agents are required to notify the student athlete's athletic director ten days prior to the signing of the contract. Violation of the statute constitutes a felony.

Iowa

The office of Secretary of State is the administrative agency governing athlete agents in Iowa. The statute (*Iowa Code Ann.* §§9A.1-.12, 722.11) applies to any person acting as an athlete representative. Any person licensed to practice as an attorney in Indiana, when negotiating a sports contract for a student athlete, is also subject to the provisions of the statute.

Potential sports agents are required to submit a written application including their educational background, training, and experience associated with representing athletes. In addition, sports agents not residing in Iowa must file an irrevocable consent to service of process with the Secretary of State. Once granted, the athlete agent's registration is valid for one year. The Secretary of State reserves the right to evaluate and investigate the accuracy of the information on the application in determining the eligibility of the sports agent. Sports agents are required to pay a $300 registration fee and any renewal fee set by the Secretary and to post a $25,000 surety bond. The statute does not limit an athlete representative's liability for damages to the amount of the surety bond.

Player/agent contract forms are subject to the approval of the Secretary of State. Sports agents must also file a schedule of fees with the Secretary; however, there are no limitations on the fees a sports agent may charge an athlete. Violation of the statute constitutes a misdemeanor. Penalties include a fine of not more than $1,000 or imprisonment of not more than one year, or both. Civil penalties are limited to a fine of not more than $10,000.

The Iowa legislature prohibits any person from providing financial incentives to a student athlete or his or her family for the purpose of inducing, encouraging, or rewarding a student athlete's enrollment in an institution of higher education or participation in an intercollegiate sporting event. A sports agent found violating this provision is guilty of an aggravated misdemeanor.

Kentucky

No specific administrative agency governs sports agents in Kentucky. Sports agents are not required to register or post surety bonds. There are also no provisions regulating player/agent contracts or sports agent fees. Prior to the expiration of a student athlete's intercollegiate eligibility, the statute (*Ky. Rev. Stat. Ann.* §§518.010–.080) prohibits any recruitment of student athletes for the purpose of signing a sports-related contract.

Violation of the statute constitutes a felony.

Louisiana

The office of Secretary of State is the administrative agency governing sports agents in Louisiana. The statute (*La. Rev. Stat. Ann.* §§4:421– 430) protects athletes eligible to participate in intercollegiate sports for a member institution of the NCAA, as well as any resident of the state involved in a team sport. Unregistered sports agents are prohibited from any direct or indirect contact with any student athlete.

Sports agents must pay a $100 annual registration fee but are not required to post a surety bond. Attorneys licensed to practice law in Louisiana are not required to register, pay annual registration fees, or submit contracts to the Secretary for approval. However, they are still subject to all the other requirements and penalties provided in the statute.

Potential sports agents are required to submit a written application listing references of persons with whom the applicant has dealt in his or her capacity as an athlete agent or in the practice of the business. Once granted, the sports agent's registration is valid for one year. The Secretary of State reserves the right to revoke a registration for violations of this statute.

Sports agents are required to file player/agent contracts entered into with Louisiana non-NCAA athletes with the Secretary. If the contract involves a Louisiana non-NCAA athlete who is a student, the sports agent must file a copy of the contract with the student athlete's athletic director. Sports agents are required to file a schedule of fees with the Secretary. Such fees may not exceed the athlete's income for any twelve-month period. Sports agents must keep detailed records containing all financial transactions performed on behalf of the athlete.

Sports agents may not give anything of value to, or enter into any agreement with, a student athlete prior to the expiration date of that athlete's intercollegiate eligibility. Sports agents committing such an offense are guilty of a misdemeanor and are subject to a fine of not more than $10,000 or imprisonment of not more than one year, or both.

Maryland

The office of Secretary of State is the administrative agency governing sports agents in Maryland. The statute (*Md. Ann. Code* art. 56, §§632–640) protects members of sports teams at institutions of higher education or high schools in the state. The statute applies to any person engaged in the representation of student athletes.

Sports agents are required to be licensed and pay annual registration fees, but no surety bond need be posted. A written application describing the sports agent's educational background and formal training relating to athlete representation must be submitted to the Secretary. Once granted, the sports agent's registration is valid for one year. The Secretary of State reserves the right to revoke a license for violations of this statute.

Player/agent contracts must be filed with the Secretary and the student athlete's athletic director. Sports agents must submit a schedule of fees to the Secretary; these are limited to a sum not exceeding the athlete's income for any twelve-month period. Sports agents must keep detailed records containing all financial transactions performed on behalf of the athlete.

Violation of the statute constitutes a misdemeanor. Penalties include a fine of not more than $10,000 or imprisonment for not more than one year, or both.

Michigan

The Michigan Department of Education is the administrative agency governing sports agents in Michigan. The statute (*Mich. Comp. Laws Ann.* §750.411e) protects any athlete eligible to engage in intercollegiate sports. Any person except for a member of the athlete's immediate family involved in the representation of these athletes is subject to the provisions of the statute.

The statute does not require a formal registration of sports agents. Nor are they required to post a surety bond or pay any fees. However, sports agents are required to adhere to specific guidelines. A sports agent may not induce a student athlete to enter into a contract prior to the expiration of the athlete's college eligibility. The statute also prohibits sports agents from offering money or valuables to a student athlete or his or her immediate family for the purpose of inducing college enrollment or athletic participation. Violation of these provisions constitutes a misdemeanor. Penalties include a fine of not more than $50,000 or an amount equal to three times the amount involved in the inducement or the agreement entered into, whichever is greater. Alternatively, the penalty could be up to a year of imprisonment, with or without fines.

Minnesota

The office of Secretary of State is the administrative agency governing sports agents in Minnesota. The statute (*Minn. Stat. Ann.* §325E.33) protects athletes eligible to participate in any intercollegiate sporting events. Sports agents are not required to register, post surety bonds, or limit their fees.

A student athlete interested in signing a professional contract must first waive college eligibility. The statute prohibits a sports agent from entering into a contract with a student athlete until the athlete has waived such college eligibility. A student athlete must submit the waiver of intercollegiate athletic eligibility to the Secretary of State and to his athletic director. Waivers become effective seven days after they are filed with the Secretary.

Minnesota is one of the few states that does not require criminal sanctions for violations for the statute. Sports agents who violate the statute may be subject to civil penalties. These penalties include a fine of not more than $10,000 or three times the amount given, offered, or promised to secure the student athlete's signature, whichever is greater.

Mississippi

The office of Secretary of State is the administrative agency governing sports agents in Mississippi. The statute (*Miss. Code Ann.* §§73-41-1–23) protects athletes enrolled in institutions of higher education and eligible to participate in intercollegiate sports. Resident athletes who are under twenty-one years of age and eligible in the future to participate in intercollegiate sports are also protected by the statute. The student athlete's institution must be a member of the NCAA or NAIA.

Potential sports agents are required to submit a written application to the Secretary, as well as pay a $50 annual registration fee and post a $100,000 surety bond. Once granted, the sports agent's registration is valid for one year. The Secretary of State, pursuant to an adjudication, reserves the right to refuse to issue or renew a registration, or revoke it, for violations of this statute. Attorneys licensed to practice law in Mississippi are not required to register with the Secretary of State or pay a registration fee. However, they are still subject to all the requirements and penalties provided in the statute.

There are no restrictions concerning player/agent contracts or sports agents' fees. Unregistered sports agents are prohibited from both direct and indirect contact with any student athlete. Registered sports agents may not intentionally enter into any agreement to represent or give anything of value to a student athlete enrolled in an institution of higher education and eligible to participate in intercollegiate sports. The penalty for such an offense is a fine of not more than $10,000 or imprisonment of not more than two years, or both. The sports agent is also liable to the aggrieved institution of higher education for damages resulting from violations of rules promulgated by the NCAA and NAIA. Sports agents must pay the aggrieved institutions any money forfeited by the institution and the cost of any lost student athlete scholarship.

North Carolina

Rather than adopt a specific student athlete statute, the North Carolina legislature requires sports agents to be subject to all the provisions of the North Carolina Investment Advisers Act. The office of Secretary of State is the administrative agency governing sports agents in North Carolina. The statute (*N.C. Gen. Stat.* §§78C-1–62) subjects sports agents to many of the common requirements associated with other agent regulatory statutes. Due to the strict provisions governing investment advisers, sports agents in North Carolina are subject to much stricter scrutiny than sports agents in other states. The Secretary is empowered with substantial authority to regulate all types of investment advisers.

The statute protects athletes with respect to professional contracts or compensatory endorsements. Any person involved in the representation of athletes is subject to the provisions of the statute. Lawyers whose performance of sports agent representation is solely incidental to the practice of their profession are exempt from the statute.

Potential sports agents are required to submit a written application listing their qualifications and business experience and pay a $200 annual registration fee. Every sports agent's registration expires on

December 31 of each year. The Secretary may require a sports agent to post surety bonds in amounts up to $100,000. Sports agents are not required to file contracts or a schedule of fees with the Secretary. All sports agents are required to file an irrevocable consent appointing the Secretary to be their attorney to receive service of any lawful process in any noncriminal suit. In addition, sports agents are required to keep detailed records of accounts, memoranda, papers, and books prescribed by the Secretary.

Sports agents who violate the statute may be guilty of a felony or subject to civil liabilities. Damages include consideration paid for the sports agent's advice and actual damages suffered by the victim, plus the costs of the action and reasonable attorney's fees.

Ohio

The office of the Ohio Attorney General is the administrative agency governing sports agents in Ohio. The statute (*Ohio Rev. Code Ann.* §§4771.01–.99) protects athletes who are enrolled in an institution of higher education and are participating in intercollegiate sports. Any person offering an agent contract to, or entering into an agent contract with, a student athlete is subject to the provisions of the statute except for a member of the student's immediate family. Attorneys representing student athletes in negotiating or soliciting an agent contract are also subject to the statute.

Sports agents are not required to register, post surety bonds, or limit their fees. Player/agent contracts must be submitted in writing to the student athlete's athletic director fourteen days prior to the signing of the contract.

Violation of the statute constitutes a first-degree misdemeanor. Penalties include a fine of not more than $1,000 or imprisonment for not more than six months, or both. Civil penalties include a fine of not more than $10,000.

Oklahoma

The office of Secretary of State is the administrative agency governing sports agents in Oklahoma. The statute (*Okla. Stat. Ann.* tit. 70, §§821.61–.71) protects athletes eligible to participate in intercollegiate sports and resident athletes engaged in a team sport. Attorneys licensed to practice law in Oklahoma are exempt from the statute provided they file an affidavit with the Clerk of the Oklahoma Supreme Court, stating their intention to represent Oklahoma student athletes.

Potential sports agents are required to submit a written application listing their experience in contract negotiations and complaint resolutions. The Secretary reserves the right to suspend or revoke a registration for violations of this statute. Unregistered athlete agents may not, directly or indirectly, contact a student athlete. Once granted, the sports agent's registration is valid for one year. Sports agents are required to pay a $1,000 annual registration fee and post a $100,000 surety bond. However, the statute does not limit the liability for damages to the amount of the surety bond.

Any player/agent contract form between a sports agent and an Oklahoma non-NCAA athlete who has never signed a professional contract must be filed with the Secretary. In addition, contracts involving student athletes must be sent to the student athlete's athletic director. Sports agents are required to file a schedule of fees charged to such Oklahoma non-NCAA athletes with the Secretary. These fees may not exceed the athlete's income for any twelve-month period. Sports agents must keep records of all financial transactions performed on behalf of the athlete.

Violation of the statute constitutes a misdemeanor. Penalties include a fine of not more than $500 or imprisonment of not more than one year, or both. Civil penalties include a fine of not more than $10,000.

Pennsylvania

Pennsylvania's statute (*Pa. Stat. Ann.* tit. 18, §7107) protects athletes who are enrolled in an institution of higher education and are eligible to participate in intercollegiate sports. The statute applies to any person engaged in the representation of student athletes.

Pennsylvania statute does not require a formal registration of sports agents. Nor does it require sports agents to pay any fees or post a surety bond. However, sports agents are required to adhere to specific guidelines. A sports agent may not induce a student athlete to enter into a contract prior to the expiration date of the athlete's college eligibility. The athlete agent is also prohibited from offering any financial incentives to a student, a member of his or her immediate family, or an employee of the student's college prior to the expiration of the student athlete's college eligibility.

Violation of this statute constitutes a first-degree misdemeanor. Penalties include a fine of not more than $10,000 or an amount equal to three times the amount given or offered to the student, his or her family, or the college employee, whichever is greater, or imprisonment for not more than a year, or both.

Tennessee

The office of the Tennessee Attorney General is the administrative agency governing sports agents in Tennessee. The statute (*Tenn. Code Ann.* §§49-7-2101–2109) protects athletes who are enrolled in an institution of higher education and are eligible to participate in intercollegiate sports. Any person engaged in the representation of student athletes is subject to the provisions of the statute. Attorneys licensed by any state who act as sports agents for student athletes are also subject to the statute.

The statute does not require a formal registration of sports agents. Sports agents are not required to pay any fees or post a surety bond and no limitations are placed on their fees. However, sports agents are required to adhere to specific guidelines. Written notice of player/agent contracts involving student athletes must be filed with the chief executive officer of the student athlete's institution of higher education within 72 hours of entering into the contract. The sports agent must follow the many contract principles outlined in the statute. The statute embodies the rules governing the NCAA. Therefore, sports agents must abide by the rules and regulation of the NCAA or face sanctions provided in the statute.

Tennessee does not hold violation of the statute as a criminal action. But sports agents violating the statute will be liable to the aggrieved institution for damages and penalties equal to three times the value of the student athlete's scholarship. Damages may also include lost revenues from ineligibility in qualifying for football bowl games and tournaments.

Texas

The office of Secretary of State is the administrative agency governing sports agents in Texas. The statute (*Tex. Rev. Civ. Stat. Ann.* art. 8871; *Tex. Civ. Prac. & Rem. Code Ann.* §§131.001–.008) protects athletes eligible to participate in intercollegiate sports and athletes who have previously participated in intercollegiate sports but have never signed a professional sports contract. Any person engaged in the representation of these athletes for compensation is subject to the provisions of the statute.

Potential sports agents are required to submit a written application listing their practical experience and educational background relating to their professional qualifications to act as a sports agent. The commission reserves the right to suspend or revoke a certificate of registration for violations of this statute. Once granted, the sports agent's registration is valid for one year. Sports agents are required to pay an annual registration fee set by the Secretary of State and post a $100,000 surety bond. However, the statute does not limit the liability for damages to the amount of the surety bond.

Player/agent contracts must be approved and on file with the Secretary. Additionally, contracts involving student athletes must be filed with the student athlete's athletic director no later than the fifth day after the contract is signed by the athlete. Sports agents are required to file a schedule of fees not exceeding the athlete's annual income for any twelve-month period. Sports agents must keep detailed records of all financial transactions performed on behalf of the athlete.

Violation of the statute constitutes a misdemeanor. Penalties include a fine of not more than $2,000 or imprisonment of not more than one year, or both. Civil penalties include a fine not to exceed $10,000.

Appendix III: Discussion Draft of Federal Sports-Agent Legislation Prepared by Congressman John Bryant of Texas

A Bill

To provide for the regulation of sports agents operating in interstate commerce and through the mails, to prevent inequitable and unfair practices in athletics, and for other purposes.

Be it enacted by the Senate and House of Representatives of the United States of America in Congress assembled,

Section 1. Short Title.

This Act may be cited as the "Professional Sports Agency Act of 1989."

Sec. 2. Findings.

The Congress finds that—

(1) the practice of sports agency entails a national public interest which makes it necessary to (A) provide for regulation and control of such practices and related matters; (B) assure that sports agents follow honest practices, adhere to professional responsibilities, and maintain educational and ethical standards; and (C) assure that clients of sports agents receive the highest levels of service consistent with licensed professional practice;

(2) current law does not provide for the licensing and regulation of independent contractors who (A) seek to recruit or solicit professional

athletes to enter into agency contracts; (B) represent professional athletes entering into professional sports services contracts or various marketing arrangements; or (C) administer the funds received by such athletes through such activities;

(3) sports (A) are enjoyed by the general public throughout the United States; (B) are affected by means of the mails and instrumentalities of interstate commerce; and (C) constitute an important part of the current of interstate commerce;

(4) sports contracts often are affected by means of the mails and instrumentalities of interstate commerce, and parties to such contracts and sports agents involved in such contracts frequently are located in diverse States; and

(5) sports agency and the solicitation of sports agency and sports contracts, marketing arrangements, and the administration of funds for professional athletes are often susceptible to impropriety, to the detriment of the general public, and athletes and athletics in general.

Sec. 3. Definitions.

As used in this Act the following terms have the following meanings:

(1) The term "active representation" means the rendering of the following services (or holding one's self out as available to render such services) to or for an athlete:

(A) Soliciting, entering into, or negotiating an agency contract.

(B) Soliciting, negotiating, or advising or consulting with an athlete regarding a sports contract.

(C) Soliciting, negotiating, or advising or consulting with an athlete regarding an advertisement, public appearance, endorsement, or similar arrangement for, on behalf of, or with respect to, an athlete.

(D) Managing or handling funds belonging to an athlete, except where all services rendered constitute (i) investment advisory services rendered by an investment advisor registered with the Securities and Exchange Commission or pursuant to the exemption under section 202(11) of the Investment Advisers Act of 1940 (15 U.S.C. 80b-2(11)); (ii) banking or trust services rendered by a bank or a licensed trust company; or (iii) legal services rendered by a licensed attorney, where all funds are held or maintained in a trust fund established by the attorney of his firm; however, nothing in this paragraph shall be interpreted to exclude attorneys from the applicability of the other provisions of this subsection.

(2) The term "agency contract" means any oral or written contract, transaction, or arrangement, pursuant to which a person is, or purports to be authorized or empowered as, a sports agent.

(3) The term "associated with" means having a legal affiliation or employment relationship.

(4) The term "athlete" means any person who participates or who is engaged in discussion which may reasonably be expected to result in participation, in professional sporting events or with professional sports teams.

(5) The term "national sports agency association" means any association of sports agents which has been approved by and registered with the Secretary as a national sports agency association pursuant to the requirements and guidelines set forth in this Act.

(6) The term "professional sporting event" means a sport contest, game, competition, or exhibition, taking place within the United States, where at least one of the participants is paid, remunerated, or compensated for the participant's services, or who may, if successful, win financial or valuable prizes (other than a reduction or elimination of college tuition).

(7) The term "professional sports team" means any organization, association, corporation, or other commercial or legal entity—

(A) engaged in regular or periodic athletic competition or exhibition which takes place within the United States as part of a league or system of inter-team competition, or

(B) which pays, remunerates, or otherwise provides compensation or financial or valuable prizes (other than a reduction or elimination of college tuition) to some or all of those participating in such competition.

(8) The term "registered agent" means a sports agent who has been registered and certified as a sports agent by an approved and registered national sports agency association, after having met that association's standards and maintained the agent's certified status in good standing.

(9) The term "Secretary" means the Secretary of Commerce.

(10) The term "sports agency" means the business of acting as a sports agent.

(11) The term "sports agent" means a person who conducts or participates in (either directly or indirectly) active representation; and such term does not include conduct or participation in active representation by any person related to an athlete by blood or by marriage.

(12) The term "sports contract" means any contract, transaction, or arrangement whereby an athlete agrees to render services as a participant or player to a professional sports team or as part of a professional sporting event.

(13) The term "State" means any State of the United States, the District of Columbia, the Commonwealth of Puerto Rico, the Virgin Islands, Guam, American Samoa, the Northern Mariana Islands, the

Trust Territory of the Pacific Islands, or any other territory or possession of the United States.

Sec. 4 Responsibilities of the Secretary of Commerce.

(a) IN GENERAL.—The Secretary shall be responsible for carrying out those functions specified as functions of the Secretary under this Act.

(b) APPOINTMENT OF STAFF.—The Secretary may, subject to applicable provisions of title 5, United States Code, appoint and fix the compensation of such attorneys, experts, and other employees as are necessary to carry out the Secretary's functions under this Act.

(c) ADMINISTRATIVE OFFICE.—The Secretary may designate (by regulation) an existing department, bureau or office, or establish a new office, within the Department of Commerce for the purpose of administering the Secretary's functions under this Act.

(d) ASSISTANCE FROM NONFEDERAL ENTITIES.—Notwithstanding any other provisions of law, in accordance with regulations which the Secretary shall promulgate under subsection (e) to prevent conflicts of interest, the Secretary may accept payment and reimbursement, in cash or in kind, from non-Federal agencies, organizations, and individuals for travel, subsistence, and other necessary expenses incurred by employees of the Secretary hired pursuant to this Act in attending meetings and conferences related to functions of the Secretary under this Act. Any such payment or reimbursement shall be deposited in the Treasury and credited to the appropriate account.

(e) PROMULGATION OF RULES AND REGULATIONS.—Any rules or regulations required or permitted to be promulgated by the Secretary under this Act shall be promulgated in accordance with section 553 of title 5, United States Code.

Sec. 5. National Sports Agency Associations.

(a) REGISTRATION OF NATIONAL SPORTS AGENCY ASSOCIATIONS.—An association of sports agencies may be registered as a national sports agency association under the terms and conditions provided in this section by filing with the Secretary an application for registration, in such form as the Secretary may prescribe, by rule. Such application shall contain the rules of the association and such other information and documents as the Secretary may prescribe, by rule, as necessary to carry out this Act.

(b) ELIGIBILITY CRITERIA FOR REGISTRATION.—An association of sports agents shall not be registered as a national sports agency association under this section unless the Secretary determines that—

(1) the association is so organized and has the capacity to be able to carry out the purposes of this Act and to comply, and to enforce compliance by its members and persons associated with its members, with the provisions of this Act, the rules and regulations promulgated pursuant to this Act, and the rules of the association;

(2) subject to section 6, the rules of the association provide that any sports agent is eligible to become a member of such association;

(3) the rules of the association assure a fair representation of its members in the selection of its directors and the administration of its affairs and provide that one or more directors shall be representative of athletes and not be, or be associated with, a sports agent;

(4) the rules of the association provide for the equitable allocation of reasonable dues, fees, and other charges among its members;

(5) the rules of the association are designed to (A) prevent fraudulent and manipulative acts and practices, promote just and equitable principles of conduct and fair dealings, and foster cooperation and coordination among athletes, sports agents, professional sports teams, sponsors or professional sporting events, and educational institutions; (B) mitigate abuses in sports contracts and services provided by sports agents; and (C) protect athletes and the public interest;

(6) the rules of the association are not designed—

(A) to permit unfair discrimination among athletes, sports agents, professional sports teams, sponsors of professional sporting events, or educational institutions, or

(B) to regulate, by virtue of any authority contained in this Act, matters not related to the purposes of this Act or the administration of the association;

(7) the rules of the association provide that (subject to any rule or order or the Secretary pursuant to section 6) its members and persons associated with such members shall be appropriately disciplined for violation of the provisions of this Act, any rules or regulations promulgated under this Act, or the rules of the association, by expulsion, suspension, limitation of activities, functions, and operations, fine, censure, suspension or prohibition from association with a member, or any other appropriate sanction;

(8) the rules of the association are consistent with subsection (d), and there are fair procedures for (A) disciplining members and persons associated with such members; (B) denial of membership to any person seeking membership; (C) barring of any person from becoming asso-

ciated with a member; and (D) prohibition or limitation by the association of any person with respect to access to services offered by the association or a member of the association;

(9) the rules of the association do not impose any burden on competition not necessary or appropriate to further the purposes of this Act; and

(10) the rules of the association do not unduly conflict with those of any previously registered association in a manner which would make compliance by a prospective member with such conflicting rules difficult.

(c) MEMBERSHIP RESTRICTED.—(1) A national sports agency association shall deny membership to any person other than a natural person or any natural person who is not, or is not associated with, a registered sports agent.

(2) A national sports agency association may or, where the Secretary directs (by order) as necessary or appropriate in the public interest or for the protection of athletes a national sports agency association, shall deny membership to any sports agent or natural person associated with a sports agent, and bar becoming associated with a member, any person who is subject to a statutory disqualification. A national sports agency association shall file notice with the Secretary not less than 30 days before admitting any person to membership or permitting any person to become associated with a member, if the association knew or, in the exercise of reasonable care, should have known that such person was subject to a statutory disqualification. Such notice shall be in such form and contain such information as the Secretary, by rule, may prescribe as necessary or appropriate in the public interest or for the protection of athletes.

(3) A national sports agency association may deny membership to, or condition the membership of, a sports agent, if—

(A) such sports agent does not meet such standards of financial responsibility or operational capability, or such sports agent, or any natural person associated with such sports agent, does not meet such standards of training, experience, and competence, as are prescribed by the rules of the association; or

(B) such sports agent, or any natural person associated with such sports agent, has engaged, and there is a reasonable likelihood that such agent or person will again engage, in acts or practices inconsistent with just and equitable rules of the association or conduct as a sports agent.

(4) A national sports agency association may examine and verify the qualifications of an applicant to become a member and any natural

persons associated with such an applicant, in accordance with procedures established by the rules of the association.

(5) A national sports agency association may bar a natural person from becoming associated with a member, or condition the membership of a member of the association of a natural person with a member, if such associated person—

(A) does not meet such standards of training, experience, and competence as are prescribed by the rules of the association; or

(B) has engaged, or there is a reasonable likelihood such person will again engage, in acts or practices inconsistent with just and equitable rules of the association or conduct of a sports agency.

(6) A national sports agency association may examine and verify the qualifications of an applicant to become a person associated with a member, in accordance with procedures established by the rules of the association. A national sports agency association may require any person associated with a member, or any class of such persons, to be registered with the association, in accordance with procedures established by the rules of the association.

(7) A national sports agency association may bar any person from becoming a member or a person associated with a member, if such person does not agree, to the extent permitted by law, to—

(A) supply the association with such information with respect to its relationship and dealings with the member or with the person associated with the member, as the case may be, as is specified in the rules of the association; and

(B) permit the examination of such person's books and records to verify the accuracy of such information.

(d) DISCIPLINARY PROCEEDINGS.—(1) In any proceeding by a national sports agency association to determine whether a member or person associated with a member should be disciplined (other than a summary proceeding conducted pursuant to paragraph (4)), the association—

(A) shall bring specific charges,

(B) shall notify such member or person of such charges,

(C) shall give such member or person an opportunity to defend against such charges, and

(D) shall keep a record of such proceeding.

(2) a determination by the association to impose a disciplinary sanction on such member or person shall be supported by a statement setting forth—

(A) any act or practice in which such member or person associated with a member has been found to have engaged, or which such member or person has been found to have omitted;

(B) the specific provisions of this Act, any rules or regulations promulgated pursuant to this Act, or of the rules of the association which the association determines to have been violated; and

(C) the sanction imposed and the reasons for such sanction.

(3) In any proceeding by a national sports agency association to determine whether a person shall be denied membership, barred from becoming associated with a member, or prohibited or limited with respect to access to services offered by the association or a member of such association (other than a summary proceeding pursuant to paragraph (4)), the association shall notify such person of the specific grounds for denial, bar, or prohibition or limitation under consideration. Such person shall be afforded an opportunity for a hearing (which hearing may consist solely of the submission of affidavits or presentation of oral arguments) regarding such specific grounds. The association shall keep a record of such proceeding. A determination by the association to deny membership, bar a person from becoming associated with a member, or prohibit or limit a person with respect to access to services offered by the association or a member of the association shall be supported by a statement setting forth the specific grounds on which such denial, bar, or prohibition or limitation is based.

(4) A national sports agency association may summarily suspend a member if the association determines that such member is in such financial or operating difficulty that the member cannot be permitted to continue to do business as a member without jeopardizing athletes, other members of the association, the public, or the association. The association shall notify the Secretary of such determination. Any person aggrieved by such summary suspension shall promptly be afforded an opportunity for a hearing (which hearing may consist solely of the submission of affidavits or presentation of oral arguments). The Secretary shall keep a record of such proceeding. The Secretary, by order, may stay any such summary suspension on the Secretary's own motion or upon application by any person aggrieved by such order, if the Secretary determines summarily or after notice and opportunity for hearing (which hearing may consist solely of the submission of affidavits or presentation of oral arguments) that such stay is consistent with the public interest and the protection of athletes.

(e) FIXED COMMISSIONS AND OTHER FEES PROHIBITED.—
No national sports agency association may impose any schedule or fix rates of commissions, allowances, discounts, or other fees to be charged by its members. A national sports agency association may require its members to disclose all such commissions, allowances, discounts or other fees to athletes or others, in such manner and form as it may prescribe.

Sec. 6. Registration and Regulation of Sports Agents.

(a) UNREGISTERED AGENT ACTIVITY PROHIBITED.—It shall be unlawful for any sports agent whose business is exclusively intrastate and who does not make use of any service of a national sports agency association to make use of the mails or any means or instrumentality of interstate commerce to effect any transaction in, or to induce or attempt to induce entry into, any agency contract or sports contract, unless such agent is registered in accordance with subsection (b).

(2) The Secretary may, by a rule or an order the Secretary deems consistent with the public interest and the protection of athletes, conditionally or unconditionally exempt from paragraph (1) any sports agent or class of sports agents specified in such rule or order.

(b) AGENCY TRANSACTIONS BY PERSONS NOT MEMBERS OF ASSOCIATIONS IS PROHIBITED.—It shall unlawful for any sports agent required to register pursuant to this Act to effect any transaction regarding any agency contract or sports contract, or to induce the formation of any sports agency contract or contract, unless such sports agent is a member of a national sports agency association, and is registered pursuant to this section.

(c) AGENT MUST MEET STANDARDS OF CAPABILITY.—(1) No registered sports agent shall effect any transaction in, or induce the formation of, any agent contract or sports contract, unless such sports agent meets standards of capability, and such sports agent and all natural persons associated with such sports agent meet such standards of training, experience, competence, and such other qualifications, as a national sports agency association or the Secretary finds necessary or appropriate in the public interest or for the protection of athletes. A national sports agency association shall establish such standards by rules which may specify that all or any part of such standards shall apply to any class of sports agents and persons associated with such sports agents.

(2) A national sports agency association may, by rule, prescribe reasonable fees and charges to defray its costs in carrying out this subsection, including fees for any test administered by such association or under its direction. The Secretary may cooperate with national sports agency associations in devising and administering tests. The Secretary may require registered sports agents and persons associated with such sports agents to pass such tests administered by or on behalf of any such association, and to pay such association reasonable fees or charges to defray the costs incurred by such association in administering such tests.

(d) ASSOCIATION REGISTRATION APPLICATION.—(1) (A) A sports agent may register with a national sports agency association by filing an application for registration. Such application shall be in writing and in such form and contain the information specified in paragraph (2) and such other information and documents concerning such sports agent and any persons associated with such sports agent as the national sports agency association or the Secretary, by rule, may prescribe as necessary or appropriate in the public interest or for the protection of athletes.

(B) Within 10 days after the date of the filing of such application, the national sports agency association shall deliver a copy of such application to the Secretary. Within 45 days after the date of the filing of such application, the national sports agency association shall grant registration to the sports agent, or request the Secretary to institute proceedings to determine whether registration should be denied. Such proceedings shall include a notice of the grounds for denials which are under consideration and shall afford an opportunity for a hearing. The proceedings shall be concluded within 120 days after the date of filing of such application. At the conclusion of such proceedings, the Secretary shall, by order, grant or deny such registration.

(C) The Secretary shall grant such registration if the Secretary finds that the requirements of this section are satisfied. The Secretary shall deny such registration, if the Secretary does not make such a finding or if the Secretary finds that, if the application were approved, the applicant's registration would be subject to suspension or revocation under section 7(a).

(2) An application filed under paragraph (1) shall contain all of the following information:

(A) The name, home address, social security number, drivers license number (and State), and professional licenses numbers and (States) and date and place of birth of the applicant.

(B) The addresses where the applicant resided during the preceding 10 years.

(C) The street and number of the building or place where the business of the applicant is to be conducted.

(D) All businesses or occupations engaged in by the applicant for at least 5 years immediately preceding the date of application.

(E) The educational background of the applicant, including names and locations of schools, dates of attendance, degrees or courses taken, transcripts and faculty references.

(F) The results of any tests or examinations required by the rules of the national sports agency association.

(G) Information regarding any arrests, indictments, convictions, administrative hearings, professional license proceedings, or civil litigation involving or regarding the applicant and all persons (except bona fide clerical employees on stated salaries) who are financially interested, either as partners, associates, bonus participants or profit sharers, in the operation of the sports agency in question, together with the amount or basis of their respective interests.

(e) SUPPORTING AFFIDAVITS REQUIRED.—Any such application must be accompanied by affidavits of at least 2 [reputable] persons who have known or have been associated with the applicant for a period of at least 5 years, and who are residents of the city or county in which the applicant has resided during that period or in which the business of the sports agent is to be conducted. Such affidavits shall state that the applicant is a person of good moral character, has a reputation for fair dealing, and has no known history of civil or criminal proceedings or litigation or administrative or licensing hearings or proceedings, except as noted in the affidavit.

(f) CHARACTER INVESTIGATION.—Upon receipt of an application under this section, a national sports agency association shall investigate the character and responsibility of the applicant and the premises designated in the application as the place in which the business of the sports agent is to be conducted. If the association requests the Secretary to institute proceedings to determine whether registration should be denied, the association shall forward to the Secretary the results of all such investigations.

(g) APPLICATION FOR SUCCESSOR AGENT.—An application of a sports agent to be formed or organized may be made by a sports agent to which the sports agent to be formed or organized is to be the successor. Such application, in such form as the national sports agency association may, by rule, prescribe, shall contain such information and documents concerning the applicant, the successor, and any persons associated with the applicant or the successor, as the national sports agency association may, by rule, prescribe as necessary or appropriate in the public interest or for the protection of athletes. The grant or denial of registration to such an applicant shall be in accordance with the procedures set forth in subsection (d)(1). If the national sports agency association approves such registration, the registration shall terminate on the forty-fifth day after the effective date of such approval, unless before such forty-fifth day the successor, in accordance with such rules and regulations as the national sports agency association may prescribe, notifies the national sports agency association that it has become the applicant.

(h) DISAPPROVAL OF PREVIOUSLY REVOKED APPLICATION.—No application shall be approved under this section if a registration of the involved sports agent had been revoked within 3 years from the date of such application.

(i) INSPECTION OF PREMISES OF SPORTS AGENT.—Within 6 months after the date of approval of an application under this section, the Secretary or, upon the authorization and direction of the Secretary, a national sports agency association of which the sports agent is a member, shall conduct an inspection of the premises where the business of the sports agent is conducted, to determine whether such business is being conducted in conformity with this Act and any rules and regulations promulgated under this Act. The Secretary may delay the inspections of any class of sports agents for a period not to exceed an additional 6 months, if the Secretary determines that such delay is necessary or appropriate.

(j) WITHDRAWAL FROM REGISTRATION.—Any registered sports agent may, upon such terms and conditions as the Secretary considers necessary or appropriate in the public interest or for the protection of athletes, withdraw from registration by filing a written notice of withdrawal with the Secretary. If a national sports agency association finds that any sports agent which is a member of such association has ceased to do business as a sports agent, the association may cancel the registration of such sports agent by giving appropriate notice to the sports agent and the Secretary. Such sports agent may make protest to the Secretary regarding such withdrawal, and the Secretary shall afford such sports agent the opportunity for a hearing.

Sec. 7. Limitations.

(a) [DISCIPLINARY ACTION].—The Secretary shall, by order, upon the recommendation of a national sports agency association or on the Secretary's own initiative, censure or place limitations on the activities, functions, or operations of any sports agent, or suspend for a period not exceeding 12 months or revoke the registration of any sports agent, if the Secretary finds, on the record after notice and opportunity for a hearing, that such censure, placing of limitations, suspension, or revocation is in the public interest and that such sports agent (whether before or after becoming a sports agent) or any person associated with such sports agent (whether before or after becoming a sports agent)—

(1) was convicted, within 10 years preceding the date of filing of any application under section 6 or at any time after such filing, of any felony or misdemeanor which the Secretary finds (A) involved agency contracts or sports contracts (or similar arrangements involving industries other than sports) and the taking of a false oath, the making of a false statement, bribery, perjury, or conspiracy to commit any such offense; (B) arose out of the conduct of the business of a sports agent, attorney, accountant, investment advisor, entertainment agent, busi-

ness agent or consultant, financial advisor, or fiduciary; or (C) involved the larceny, theft, robbery, extortion, forgery, counterfeiting, fraudulent concealment, embezzlement, fraudulent conversion, or misappropriation of funds;

(2) is permanently or temporarily enjoined by order, judgment, or decree of any court of competent jurisdiction from acting as a sports agent or from engaging in or continuing any conduct or practice in connection with conducting business as a sports agent, or in connection with the establishment or conduct of any sports contract;

(3) has willfully violated any provision of this Act, any rule or regulation promulgated under this Act, any rule of a national sports agency association, or any rule of the Secretary promulgated under this Act;

(4) has willfully aided, abetted, counseled, commanded, induced, or procured the violation by any person of any provision of this Act, any rule or regulation promulgated under this Act, any rule of a national sports agency association, or any rule promulgated by the Secretary under this Act, or has failed reasonably to supervise (in order to prevent violations of such statutes, rules, and regulations) any person who has committed such a violation, if such other person is subject to the supervision of such sports agent or any person associated with such sports agent; or

(5) is subject to an order of the Secretary entered pursuant to this subsection which bars or suspends the right of such person to be associated with a sports agent. For the purposes of paragraph (4), no person shall be considered to have failed reasonably to supervise any other person, if there have been established procedures, and a system for applying such procedures, which would reasonably be expected to prevent and detect (insofar as practicable) any such violation by such other person, and if such person has reasonably discharged the duties and obligations incumbent upon such person by reason of such procedures and system without reasonable cause to believe that noncompliance with such procedures and system exists.

(b) SUSPENSION OF REGISTRATION PENDING FINAL DETERMINATION OF REVOCATION OF REGISTRATION.—Pending a final determination whether any registration under this section shall be revoked, the Secretary may, by order, suspend such registration, if such suspension appears to the Secretary, after notice and opportunity for a hearing, to be necessary or appropriate in the public interest or for the protection of athletes.

(c) DISCIPLINARY ACTION.—(1) The Secretary shall, by order, upon the recommendation of a national sports agency association or on the Secretary's own initiative, censure or place limitations on the activities or functions of any person associated or seeking to become associated with a sports agent, or suspend for a period not exceeding 12 months or bar any such person from being associated with a sports agent, if the Secretary finds, on the record after notice and an opportunity for a hearing, that such censure, placing of limitations, suspension, or bar is in the public interest and that such person has been convicted of any offense specified in subsection (a)(1) or has committed or omitted any act or omission specified in subsection (a)(3) or (4).

(2) It shall be unlawful for any person as to whom such an order is in effect willfully to become, or to be, associated with a sports agent, without the consent of the Secretary.

(3) It shall be unlawful for any sports agent to permit such a person to become, or remain, a person associated with such sports agent without the consent of the Secretary, if such sports agent knew, or in the exercise of reasonable care should have known, of such order.

Appendix IV: TACTRUST Agreement

TRUST AGREEMENT to establish a trust to be known as TACTRUST by and among the bank, trust company or other fiduciary whose name and address is indicated on Schedule "A" hereof, the individual athletes whose name or names and addresses are set forth on Schedule "B" hereof, and The Athletics Congress of the USA, Inc. whose address is 200 South Capitol Avenue, Suite 140, Indianapolis, Indiana 46225.

    1.0 PREAMBLE. The individual athletes may receive (a) athletic funds by virtue and as a result of athletic activity or (b) sponsorship payments and benefits as a result of sponsorship activity. The individual athletes wish to be eligible under IAAF rules to enter and compete in international amateur athletic competition notwithstanding their receipt of such funds, payments and benefits. The Athletics Congress of the USA, Inc., as the national governing body in the United States for Athletics, pursuant to the Amateur Sports Act of 1978 (36 USC 371) has obtained the approval of the International Amateur Athletic Federation of the trust to be created hereby as a method of protecting the eligibility of the athletes of the United States.

    2.0 DEFINITIONS. As used in this trust agreement, the following terms shall have the meanings set forth herein:

    2.1 "TACTRUST" shall mean the trust fund created by this trust agreement the full name of which shall be "TAC/USA Athletes' Trust."

    2.2 "TAC/USA" shall mean The Athletics Congress of the USA, Inc.

    2.3 "Athlete beneficiary" or "athlete beneficiaries" shall mean any and all individual athletes party to this trust agreement and any corporate party to this trust agreement identified as an athlete beneficiary on either the signature page of this trust agreement or any amendments thereto provided said corporate party has fully complied with paragraph "20" hereof.

2.4 "IAAF" shall mean the International Amateur Athletic Federation.

2.5 "Trustee" shall mean the bank, trust company, or other fiduciary named on Schedule "A" hereof.

2.6 "Eligibility" shall mean the right under applicable TAC/USA and IAAF rules of an athlete to represent and compete on behalf of the United States of America in the Olympic Games, the Pan-American Games, IAAF World Championships and to compete in other international athletic meetings involving the athletes of two or more countries.

2.7 "Pro-rata" shall mean the equal allocation among the athlete beneficiaries of TACTRUST of the expenses and income of TACTRUST which allocation shall be apportioned among all athlete beneficiaries of TACTRUST based on the average monthly balance (that is to say, the balance at the beginning of each month plus the balance at the end of each month divided by two) in each athlete beneficiary's account the TACTRUST calculated on a calendar year basis.

2.8 "Domestic Competition" shall mean an athletic competition in which all of the participating athletes are citizens of the United States or if citizens of countries other than the United States participate such athletes are bona fide registered athletes of TAC/USA.

2.9 "International Competition" shall mean an athletic competition in which citizens from more than one country participate and all non-U.S. citizens are not bona-fide registered athletes of TAC/USA.

2.11 "Sponsorship payments or benefits" shall mean money, property or other benefits received by an athlete pursuant to the TAC/USA Athlete Sponsorship Program.

2.12 Except for the foregoing definitions, any term, word, or phrase used in this trust agreement which is defined in Article 2 of the TAC/USA By-Laws shall have the same definition as provided therein. Any such definition shall and may continue to be amended as, if and when any amendment is effected in the definitions contained in the said By-Laws.

3.0 PURPOSE. The purposes of this trust agreement are to:

(i) create a trust fund under IAAF and TAC/USA rules which provides for (a) the deposit of (i) athletic funds and sponsorship payments or benefits by an athlete beneficiary and (ii) other monies the deposit of which is provided for herein or approved by TAC/USA and (b) a method of withdrawals of principal and income therefrom so that for so long as the athlete beneficiary is a party to this trust agreement, the eligibility shall not be impaired solely by virtue of payments into or withdrawals from TACTRUST by the athlete; and

(ii) furnish a model private trust agreement for any athlete who does not wish to become an athlete beneficiary of TACTRUST (or who might wish to become an athlete beneficiary thereof for only a part of the funds and payments received by such athlete) but who nevertheless does wish to establish a private trust agreement for all or part of such funds and payments to be received, which private trust agreement will protect the eligibility of such athlete to the same extent and in the same manner as such protection is afforded by TACTRUST.

4.0 CREATION OF TACTRUST. The parties hereto hereby establish TACTRUST and the trustee hereby accepts a trust consisting solely of such property as shall be paid or delivered to the trustee by or on behalf of each athlete beneficiary. The trustee shall hold the trust fund in trust and manage and administer it in accordance with the terms and provisions of this trust agreement. The trustee shall accept no property other than that paid or delivered to it pursuant to paragraph 5.0 et seq. hereof.

5.0 ATHLETE BENEFICIARIES AND PAYMENTS INTO TACTRUST. The following provisions describe who may be an athlete beneficiary of TACTRUST and the athletic funds, sponsorship payments and other property which may be accepted into or be subject to TACTRUST.

5.1 Any athlete in whose name a validly issued current TAC/USA registration card has been issued, may, while a TAC/USA registered athlete in good standing, become an athlete beneficiary of TACTRUST. No person attending a NCAA school may become a TACTRUST athlete beneficiary until the college or university class of which he or she is a member is graduated unless such person has not competed in a varsity sports program of that school for a period of 12 consecutive months and has declared that he or she will not compete in future in any such program.

5.2 Only the following property shall be paid or delivered to the trustee by or for an athlete beneficiary and the trustee shall not accept any other property in TACTRUST.
  (i) Athletic funds received by an athlete beneficiary for participating in a domestic competition sanctioned by TAC/USA;
  (ii) Athletic funds received by an athlete beneficiary for participating in an international competition sanctioned by either TAC/USA or the national governing body having jurisdiction in the venue of such competition;
  (iii) Athletic funds received by an athlete beneficiary prior to January 1, 1982 for participating in a domestic or international competition subject to the approval of TAC/USA.
  (iv) Property or funds received by an athlete beneficiary as a donation, provided such donations are permissible under IAAF rules and are approved by TAC/USA.
  (v) Payments or benefits received by an athlete beneficiary resulting from an Athlete Sponsorship Program arrangement approved by TAC/USA.
  (vi) Property received by an athlete registered or wishing to be registered with TAC/USA from any source whatsoever which if not deposited into TACTRUST would give rise to an impairment of such athlete's eligibility provided, however, that TAC/USA first approves the use of TACTRUST for such purposes.

5.3 All monies paid or delivered to the trustee pursuant to paragraph 5.2 shall be paid and delivered by good check to the trustee and shall represent the entire sum of money payable to the athlete beneficiary with respect to the transaction involved.

5.4 The athlete beneficiary shall give TAC/USA prompt notice of any proposed payment into TACTRUST. TAC/USA may object to such payment by notifying the athlete beneficiary and the trust of its objections within thirty (30) days of its actual receipt of such notice. In the event TAC/USA objects to payment the trustee shall not accept it into TACTRUST.

5.5 As to any payments which are accepted by the trustee into TACTRUST, the athlete beneficiary for whose account said payment is accepted, herein assigns, conveys, transfers, and delivers to the trustee said funds to be administered pursuant to TACTRUST for the purposes herein stated.

6.0 ATHLETE BENEFICIARY ACCOUNT. The trustee shall administer the payments received into TACTRUST as follows:

6.1 The trustee (and not TAC/USA) shall administer TACTRUST.

6.2 Each athlete beneficiary shall be assigned by the trustee a TAC-TRUST account number. All payments received by the trustee for the benefit of the athlete beneficiary will be credited to such an account. Any income of TACTRUST allocated to the athlete beneficiary shall also be credited hereto. All withdrawals by the athlete beneficiary of funds from TACTRUST and the pro-rata share of the administrative expenses of TACTRUST shall be deducted therefrom.

6.3 The trustee shall not be required to segregate the funds allocable to each athlete beneficiary's account from the funds of other athlete beneficiaries. The trustee may commingle the entire funds paid into TACTRUST and exercise the investment and the other powers conferred upon the trustee on the entire corpus of TACTRUST or such part of it as it deems appropriate.

6.4 All earnings, income, gains, expenses, losses, fees, and other costs allocable to TACTRUST shall be shared on a pro-rata basis by all the athlete beneficiaries.

6.5 The trustee shall have the right to cause the retention in each athlete beneficiary's account of such sums as it deems appropriate to enable the athlete beneficiary to meet his or her pro-rata share of the expenses and costs of the administration of TAC-TRUST.

6.6 Unless a different time period is otherwise agreed to between the trustee and TAC/USA, the athlete beneficiary and TAC/USA shall be sent monthly reports by the trustee of transaction activity in the account of each athlete beneficiary not later than ten (10) days after the close of each calendar month.

7.0 WITHDRAWALS OF PRINCIPAL, TRANSFERS, AND DISTRIBUTION OF INCOME. The trustee and each athlete beneficiary may deal with the account standing in the name of the athlete beneficiary in the following manner:

7.1 Amounts due for income taxes which arise out of a payment into or out of TACTRUST for the account or the benefit of an athlete beneficiary may be withdrawn from the principal of the TACTRUST allocated to the account of the affected athlete beneficiary.

7.2 The income of TACTRUST shall be computed on all accrual basis. Within 105 days after the close of each calendar year, the trustee shall allocate the income of TACTRUST to the athlete beneficiaries on a pro-rata basis. The trustee shall apportion the income of TACTRUST to the basis of income received and accrued to that date. The income to be allocated to any athlete beneficiary of TACTRUST shall be the income from the last income allocation made before the death of the athlete beneficiary. The trustee shall not be required to prorate any income payment to the date of the athlete beneficiary's death.

7.3 The athlete beneficiary may withdraw all or any part of the principal sum and any interest or income thereto applicable to the account of the athlete beneficiary by requesting the trustee to pay the same in accordance with Schedule "C" hereof. No withdrawal pursuant to this paragraph 7.3 shall be made prior to obtaining the written consent of TAC/USA to said withdrawal, which consent shall be given or withheld by TAC/USA in its sole discretion applied consistently under TAC/USA and IAAF rules. The trustee shall pay the requested sum only after TAC/USA's consent thereto is given.

7.4 The athlete beneficiary may withdraw all or any part of the principal sum standing in his or her account by requesting the trustee to pay all or part of said principal sum to the athlete beneficiary or his or her designee without the written consent of TAC/USA for said withdrawal. The trustee shall make such payments only if the athlete beneficiary states in the written request therefor that "This withdrawal is made without the consent of TAC/USA, and that it is understood that the withdrawal will result in proceedings to impair his or her eligibility." It shall be a rebuttable presumption that a withdrawal without TAC/USA consent was for a purpose not in conformity with applicable rules and regulations of TAC/USA and IAAF subject to review of the reasons for said withdrawal at a hearing which TAC/USA institutes to review the athlete beneficiary's eligibility. The trustee shall forthwith notify TAC/USA of any withdrawal at the time thereof by an athlete beneficiary pursuant to this paragraph 7.4.

7.5 The athlete beneficiary initially may establish or may transfer all or any part of the principal in his or her account to a private trust created for a purpose similar to TACTRUST (the "private trust") in which TAC/USA is also a "notify and consent" party as provided in TACTRUST. A copy of such proposed private trust agreement shall be sent to TAC/USA. Upon the consent of TAC/USA to such private trust and the actual deposit therein or transfer thereto of all or part of the principal hereof, there shall be no impairment of the athlete's eligibility. All private trusts shall have as one of the trustees thereof a bank, trust company or other institution customarily acting in such capacity. This requirement may be waived by TAC/USA on good cause shown. The name of all private trusts shall be substantially as follows: "TAC/USA and (name of trustee or athlete beneficiary), Athlete's Private Trust" and no acronym thereof shall be utilized by any party thereto.

8.0 ACTS OF REVOCATION AND TERMINATION. The interest of an athlete beneficiary shall be revoked or terminated in the account standing in his or her name in TACTRUST (or any private trust) upon the happening of any of the following:

8.1 Upon the death of an athlete beneficiary the interest of said athlete beneficiary shall terminate in TACTRUST and the then entire account standing in the name of the deceased athlete beneficiary shall be paid to the person named in Schedule "D" hereof, and if no person is named therein then to the legal representative of such athlete beneficiary. Any private trust may contain provisions in its initial form or by subsequent amendment which in the event of the death of the athlete beneficiary (a) allows the trust to continue, (b) names successor beneficiaries therein, and (c) terminates the role of TAC/USA in such trust.

8.2 If an athlete beneficiary (a) declares himself or herself in writing to be (i) a professional athlete, (ii) an athlete not wishing to retain eligibility, or (iii) an athlete no longer interested in competing; (b) surrenders for life his or her membership in TAC/USA; (c) is suspended for life as a TAC/USA athlete member; (d) makes any withdrawal of principal pursuant to paragraph 7.4. hereof; (e) accepts athletic funds unless the same are contributed to a trust as provided hereunder; or (f) after January 1, 1983, knowingly competes in an international athletic competition held within the United States not sanctioned by TAC/USA, the interest of the athlete beneficiary in TACTRUST shall be deemed to have been revoked and the trust terminated with respect to said athlete beneficiary. Upon certification to the trustee by TAC/USA of the happening of any one of such events all monies then in the account of such athlete beneficiary shall be paid by the trustee to the athlete beneficiary. The trustee shall have no responsibility under this paragraph except to act in accordance with the certificate of TAC/USA.

8.3 The entire right to receive all monies in the account of the athlete beneficiary shall be vested in the athlete beneficiary of a TACTRUST account subject only to the provisions of this trust agreement and nothing contained herein shall give TAC/USA or the trustee or either of them any right to any part of TAC-

TRUST, the income or increase thereof, or any residuary rights therein, except that nothing contained herein shall be deemed to prohibit the trustee from receiving its compensation from the corpus of TACTRUST as provided in this trust agreement.

8.4 It is the intent of TAC/USA to create TACTRUST and to provide for payments into and out of TACTRUST (and any private trust) which will permit the most favorable incidents of income taxation permissible under existing law and regulations. To the extent that this instrument requires amendment or to the extent any private trust requires provisions more suitable to the needs of any particular beneficiary thereof, TAC/USA will effect said amendment or permit the creation of a private trust provided said amendment or transfer trust provisions are allowed by IAAF. TAC/USA makes no representation as to the tax consequences of any payment into or out of TACTRUST or any private trust.

9.0 TAC/USA AND THE ATHLETE BENEFICIARIES OF TAC-TRUST. The following provisions are applicable to the relationship of TAC/USA and the TACTRUST athlete beneficiaries:

9.1 TAC/USA shall have no role in the administration of TAC-TRUST or any private trust except to certify that payments into or out of the particular trust involved are permitted by IAAF and TAC/USA rules.

9.2 TAC/USA shall receive no compensation for its services to or in connection with TACTRUST either directly or indirectly from TACTRUST, the trustee or any athlete beneficiary nor shall any employee, agent, attorney, division or subsidiary of TAC/USA receive direct or indirect compensation therefor from TACTRUST, the trustee or any athlete beneficiary.

9.3 TAC/USA shall not be liable to the trustee or the athlete beneficiary for any loss suffered by TACTRUST or of any impairment of eligibility of an athlete beneficiary resulting from its consent to any payment made into or out of TACTRUST for the account of the athlete beneficiary. Such consent by TAC/USA shall merely signify that based upon the facts certified to TAC/USA at the time of said consent, the payment was in conformity with applicable TAC/USA, IAAF, or TACTRUST rules, regulations or provisions. If the facts certified to TAC/USA are found to be true by TAC/USA after investigation, TAC/USA shall use its best efforts to protect the athlete beneficiary's eligibility before any international body.

9.4 Any withdrawal by an athlete beneficiary not approved by TAC/USA pursuant to 7.4 hereof may result in the loss of eligibility of the said athlete beneficiary under applicable TAC/USA or IAAF rules, but nothing contained herein shall be deemed to deprive an athlete beneficiary of his or her rights pursuant to the By-Laws of TAC/USA.

10.0 INVESTMENT POWERS OF TRUSTEE. In addition to any powers which the trustee may have under applicable law, the trustee shall have and in its sole and absolute discretion may exercise from time to time and at any time the following powers and authority with respect to TACTRUST:

a. To invest and reinvest trust funds, together with any other assets held by the trustee for the benefit of TACTRUST and its athlete beneficiaries, in shares of stock (whether common or preferred), money market funds, mutual funds, certificates of deposit, IRA funds or other evidences of indebtedness, unsecured or secured by mortgages on real or personal property wheresoever situated (including any part interest in a bond and mortgage or note and mortgage, whether insured or uninsured), and any other property, or part interest in property, real or personal, foreign or domestic, without any duty to diversify and without regard to any restriction placed upon fiduciaries by any present or future applicable law, administrative regulation, rule of court or court decision.

b. To sell, convey, redeem, exchange, grant options for the purchase or exchange of, or otherwise dispose of, any real or personal property, at public or private sale, for cash or upon credit, with or without security, without obligation on the part of any person dealing with the trustee to see to the application of the proceeds of or to inquire into the validity, expediency, or propriety of any such disposition;

c. To borrow from any lender (including the trustee in its individual capacity) money, in any amount and upon any terms and conditions, for purposes of this agreement, and to pledge or mortgage any property held in TACTRUST to secure the repayment of any such loan;

d. To employ in the management of TACTRUST suitable agents, without liability for any loss occasioned by any such agents selected by the trustee with reasonable care, and to compensate any such agent from TACTRUST funds without diminution of or charging against the commissions or compensation due the trustee hereunder.

e. To consult with counsel, who may be counsel to TAC/USA, on matters relating to the management of the TACTRUST, without liability for taking or refraining from taking action in accordance with the opinion of such counsel; and

f. To do all other acts that the trustee may deem necessary or proper to carry out any of the powers or duties set forth herein or otherwise in the best interest of TACTRUST.

11.0 TAXES, EXPENSES, AND COMPENSATION OF TRUSTEE.

a. The trustee, without direction from any party hereto, shall pay out of the principal of TACTRUST all taxes imposed or levied with respect to TACTRUST and, in its discretion, may contest the validity or amount of any tax, assessment, claim, or demand respecting TACTRUST or any part thereof.

b. The trustee, without direction from any party hereto, shall pay from TACTRUST the reasonable expenses and compensation of counsel and all other expenses of managing and administering TACTRUST, provided that no compensation to or expense of counsel for TAC/USA shall be paid by the trustee from TACTRUST. All expenses paid pursuant to this paragraph "11.0" hereof shall be paid from the principal of TACTRUST except to the extent that the trustee in its discretion shall determine otherwise. The trustee shall receive such compensation for its services as from time to time shall be agreed upon, without necessity of application to or approval by any court. Until otherwise determined by the trustee and TAC/USA, such compensation shall be as set forth in Schedule "E" hereof. All compensation payable to the trustee shall be paid from the principal of TACTRUST unless the trustee in its discretion shall determine otherwise.

12.0 PRINCIPAL AND INCOME ALLOCATION. Allocation as between principal and income accounts shall be as follows: There shall be credited to principal, to the extent that the same shall constitute principal, all funds received by the trustee from an athlete beneficiary, profits realized on the sale or exchange of investments, and stock dividends or other distributions. There shall be charged against income all expenses properly chargeable to income, including any taxes and assessments chargeable to the income of TACTRUST pursuant to any statute or regulation.

12.1 Dividends or other distributions payable in the stock of the corporation authorizing and declaring the same, however, shall constitute principal and the trustee may apportion extraordinary dividends or other corporate distribution payable in cash or property other than the stock of the corporation authorizing and declaring the same, liquidating dividends, arrears of dividends on preferred stocks, property received in reorganization and other like receipts not constituting ordinary income to principal or income or in part to both in the sole judgment and discretion of the trustee. Premiums paid for the purchase of investments for TACTRUST shall not be amortized.

13.0 TRUSTEE'S LIABILITY. The trustee shall not be liable for the making, retention, or sale of any investment or reinvestment made by it as herein provided nor for any loss to or diminution of TACTRUST, except due to its own negligence, willful misconduct, or lack of good faith. The trustee shall have no liability or responsibility to investigate the truth or falsity of any certificate, content, approval or request received by it from TAC/USA or an athlete beneficiary.

14.0 ACCOUNTS. The trustee shall keep accurate and detailed accounts of all its receipts, investments and disbursements under this agreement. Such person or persons as TAC/USA shall designate shall be allowed to inspect the trustee's account relating to the TACTRUST upon request at any reasonable time during the business hours of the trustee. Within 90 days after the close of the fiscal year of TACTRUST or of the removal or resignation of the trustee as provided by this agreement, the trustee shall file with TAC/USA a written account of its transactions relating to TACTRUST during the period from the submission of its last such account to the close of the fiscal year or the date of the trustee's resignation or removal. Unless TAC/USA shall have filed with the trustee written exceptions of objections to any such account within 60 days after receipt thereof, TAC/USA shall be deemed to have approved such account; and in such case, the trustee shall be forever released and discharged with respect to all matters and things embraced in such account as though such account had been settled by court of competent jurisdiction in an action or preceeding to which all persons having a beneficial interest in TACTRUST were parties. However, should any question be raised at any time by any athlete beneficiary regarding his or her proper share of the income from TACTRUST, the trustee will use its best efforts to supply TAC/USA with the information necessary to resolve the inquiry. Nothing contained in this agreement shall deprive the trustee of the right to have a judicial settlement of its accounts.

15.0 RESIGNATION OR REMOVAL OF TRUSTEE.

    a. The trustee may resign at any time upon 90 days' written notice to TAC/USA, or upon shorter notice if acceptable to TAC/USA. TAC/USA, by action of its Board of Directors, may remove the trustee at any time upon 120 days written notice to the trustee, or upon shorter notice if acceptable to the trustee. In the event it resigns or is removed, the trustee shall have its accounts settled as provided in this agreement.

    b. Upon the resignation or removal of the trustee, TAC/USA, by action of its Board of Directors, shall appoint a successor trustee to act hereunder after the effective date of such removal or resignation. However, TAC/USA shall not appoint as successor trustee either itself or any athlete beneficiary of TACTRUST. Each successor trustee shall have the powers and duties conferred upon the trustee in this agreement, and the term "trustee" as used in this agreement shall be deemed to include any successor trustee. Upon designation or appointment of a successor trustee, the trustee shall transfer and deliver all trust funds to the successor trustee, reserving such sums as the trustee shall deem necessary to defray its expenses in settling its accounts, to pay any of its compensation due and unpaid, and to discharge any obligation of TACTRUST for which the trustee may be liable; but if the sums so reserved are not sufficient for these purposes, the trustee shall be entitled to recover the amount of any deficiency from a successor trustee. When all TACTRUST funds shall have been transferred and delivered to the successor trustee and the accounts of the trustee have been settled as provided in these agreements, the trustee shall be released and discharged from all further accountability or liability for TACTRUST and shall not be responsible in any way for the further disposition of TACTRUST or any part thereof.

16.0 COMMUNICATIONS.

    a. Any action required by any provision of this agreement to be taken by TAC/USA may be evidenced by a resolution of its Board of Directors certified to the trustee by the secretary or an assistant secretary or equivalent officer of TAC/USA and the trustee shall be fully protected in relying on any resolution so certified to it. Any action of TAC/USA including any approval of or exception to the trustee's accounts with respect to TACTRUST, may be evidenced by a certificate signed by the officer of TAC/USA authorized to do so by resolution by its Board of Directors and the trustee shall be fully protected in relying upon such certificate. The trustee may accept any writing signed by an officer of TAC/USA as proof of any fact or matter that it deems necessary or desirable to have established in the administration of TAC-TRUST and the trustee shall be fully protected in relying upon the statements in writing. The trustee shall be entitled conclusively to rely upon any written notice, instruction, direction, certificate, or other communication believed by it to be genuine and to be signed by the proper person or persons, and the trustee shall be under no duty to make investigation or inquiry as to the truth or accuracy of any statement contained therein.

b. Until notice be given to the contrary, communications to the trustee shall be sent to it at its office designated on Schedule "A" hereof; communications to athlete beneficiaries or their legal representatives shall be sent to the address furnished to the trustee by the athlete beneficiary and communications to TAC/USA shall be sent to it at the address set forth in this agreement.

17.0 AMENDMENT. TAC/USA expressly reserves the right at any time and from time to time to amend this agreement and the trust created thereby to any extent that it may deem advisable, provided, however, that such amendment shall not increase the duties or responsibilities of the trustee without its consent thereto in writing, and provided further that no such amendment shall be made which retroactively entitles TAC/USA to earn a fee or other compensation out of the funds constituting TACTRUST or otherwise retroactively reduces the share of any athlete beneficiary to the principal or income of TACTRUST. Such amendment shall become effective upon delivery to the trustee of a written instrument of amendment, duly executed and acknowledged by TAC/USA, and accompanied by a certified copy of a resolution of its Board of Directors authorizing such amendment. An athlete beneficiary of TACTRUST or any private trust pursuant thereto may object to any amendment of the bylaws of TAC/USA (as they affect TACTRUST) or any amendment to TACTRUST by notifying TAC/ USA within 30 days of such amendment. If the athlete beneficiary does not waive such objection, the following rules shall apply:

a) For so long as the athlete remains eligible, there shall be no further payments into or out of the trust for the account of said athlete beneficiary and the amendment shall be ineffective with respect to the funds in the account of said athlete beneficiary;

b) Any funds thereafter received by the athlete may be placed by him or her in a new TACTRUST account which shall be governed by the amendment, and payments into and out of said account shall be permitted in accordance therewith.

c) Upon the cessation of the athlete beneficiary's eligibility or any act of revocation or termination pursuant to paragraph "8.0" hereof, the entire balance, without penalty, standing in the account of the athlete beneficiary in the "frozen" TACTRUST and any other TACTRUST in which said athlete has an interest shall be paid to such athlete in accordance with the terms of the trust involved.

18.0 PROHIBITION OF ASSIGNMENT OF INTEREST. Without the consent of TAC/USA the funds of any athlete beneficiary in his or her account and any interest, right or claim in or to any part of TACTRUST or any payment therefrom shall not be assignable, transferable, or subject to sale, mortgage, pledge, hypothecation, commutation, anticipation, garnishment, attachment, execution, or levy or any kind, and the trustee shall not recognize any attempt to assign, transfer, sell, mortgage, pledge, hypothecate, commute, or anticipate the same, except to the extent required by law.

19.0 MISCELLANEOUS.

a. This agreement shall be interpreted, construed, and enforced, and the trust hereby created shall be administered, in accordance with the laws of the state where the trustee is located.

b. The captions of the Articles of this trust agreement are placed herein for convenience only and the agreement is not to be construed by reference thereto.

c. This agreement shall bind and inure to the benefit of the successors and assigns of TAC/USA, the trustee, and each athlete beneficiary, respectively.

d. This agreement may be executed in any number of counterparts, each of which shall be deemed to be an original, but all of which together shall constitute but one instrument, which may be sufficiently evidenced by counterpart.

e. The effective date of this trust agreement shall be as to TAC/USA and the trustee the date set forth next to their signatures and as to each athlete beneficiary, the date said athlete beneficiary causes funds to be paid into TACTRUST for his or her account.

20.0 ATHLETE CORPORATIONS. The athlete beneficiary may enter into an agreement with a corporation to receive all or some of the funds described in paragraphs "1.0" and "5.2" of TACTRUST (the "athlete's corporation.") The following provisions shall apply with respect thereto:

a. The relationship of the athlete to the athlete's corporation shall not modify or diminish the jurisdiction over the athlete of either the Athletic Congress of the USA, Inc. or the International Amateur Athletic Federation. The athlete shall be fully responsible for all acts of the athlete's corporation as a party to TACTRUST the same as if all such acts were the personal acts of the athlete and the athlete shall be chargeable with knowledge of all such acts without regard to the fact that the person or persons performing such acts for the athlete's corporation are persons other than the athlete.

b. Any athlete's corporation wishing to become an "athlete beneficiary" as defined in TACTRUST shall, as a condition of maintaining such status, provide to the TAC/USA, upon its incorporation as soon as thereafter as possible, a copy of any service or employment agreement with an individual athlete and a copy of any stockholders agreements. The athlete corporation shall also agree that, during the term of TACTRUST it will report to TAC/USA any material change in any of the above-described documents or in its structure and organization.

c. No person declared to be ineligible to compete as an athlete under any applicable TAC/USA of IAAF rule shall be entitled to be a shareholder, officer, or director of an athlete's corporation.

d. With respect to an athlete's corporation, TAC/USA makes no representation as to either the tax consequences of its being a party to TACTRUST or any deposits or withdrawals made by it into or out of TACTRUST. TAC/USA shall have no responsibility to any athlete by virtue of any acts, omissions, or defalcations of any person acting for an athlete's corporation it being understood that consent of TAC/USA to an athlete's corporation being an athlete beneficiary of TACTRUST is solely for the benefit of the individual athlete and shall not deemed to enlarge TAC/USA responsibilities in any manner whatsoever.

IN WITNESS WHEREOF, the corporate parties hereto have caused this agreement to be executed in their respective names by their duly authorized officers under their corporate seals and the individual parties hereto have executed this agreement and affixed their seals.

The Athletics Congress of the U.S.A.

Inc.,

by _____

The Trustee

(Signing on Schedule "A" hereof)

by _____

The Athlete Beneficiary

(Signing on Schedule "B" hereof)

Notes

Introduction

1. "Palmer Adds New Charges Against Walters, Bloom," *Sports Industry News,* July 29, 1988, p. 239.
2. See, e.g., Fiffer, "Two Sports Agents Convicted of Fraud and Racketeering," *New York Times,* April 14, 1989, A-1, col. 1, A-31, col. 3.
3. Johnson and Reid, "Some Offers They Couldn't Refuse," *Sports Illustrated,* May 21, 1979, p. 35.
4. Gup, "Playing to Win in Vegas," *Time,* April 3, 1989, p. 57.
5. Oliver Williamson, *Markets and Hierarchies* (New York: The Free Press, 1975).
6. Bannon, "Ex-Agent: 'No Clean Programs,'" *USA Today,* Dec. 17, 1987, C-1, col. 4.
7. John Gorman, "'Agent Threatened Me': Bears' Douglass," *Chicago Tribune,* March 16, 1989, sec. 4, p. 1, col. 3. See discussion in next chapter.
8. See Chapter 5.

Chapter 1

1. Leigh Steinberg, "Time to Revise Game Rules," *Sporting News,* Nov. 16, 1987, p. 10.
2. Fiffer, "Two Sports Agents Convicted of Fraud and Racketeering," *New York Times,* April 14, 1989, A-1, col. 1, A-31, col. 2.
3. Robert Ruxin, *An Athlete's Guide to Agents* (Lexington, Mass.: Stephen Greene, 1989), p. 29.
4. Richard D. Schultz, speech to Sports Lawyers Association, Washington, D.C., May 12, 1989.
5. Interview with Reginald Wilkes, Sept. 11, 1989.
6. Jeffrey Z. Rubin and Frank E. A. Sander, "When Should We Use Agents?: Direct vs. Representative Negotiation," *Negotiation Journal,* Oct. 1988, p. 401.
7. Ruxin, *Athlete's Guide,* p. 18.
8. *Ibid.*

9. *Ibid.*

10. House Select Committee on Professional Sports, *Inquiry into Professional Sports, Final Report: H.R. 1786,* 94th Cong., 2d sess. (1977), p. 70.

11. John Culver, speech to Sports Lawyers Association, Washington, D.C., May 12, 1989.

12. See Donald E. Biederman et al., *Law and Business of the Entertainment Industries* (Dover, Mass.: Auburn House, 1987), p. 471.

13. *Ibid.*

14. Kashif, speech to Black Entertainment and Sports Lawyers Association, Antigua, British West Indies, Nov. 3, 1989.

15. There have been a number of scholarly articles examining various aspects of this field. All give an overview of the role of the athlete agent. See e.g., "The Agent-Athlete Relationship in Professional and Amateur Sports: The Inherent Potential for Abuse and the Need for Regulation," *Buffalo Law Review* 30 (1981): 815; "Agents of Professional Athletes," *New England Law Review* 15 (1980): 545; "Attorneys and the California Athlete Agencies Act: The Toll of the Bill," *Hastings Communication and Entertainment Law Journal* 7 (1985): 551; Benitez, "Of Sports, Agents, and Regulations—The Need for a Different Approach," *Entertainment and Law Journal* 3 (1986): 199; Burleigh, "Sports Law and Representation: More Agents Than Players in Lucrative Field?," *Chicago Daily Law Bulletin* 133 (Oct. 7, 1987): 1, col. 4; Massey, "The Crystal Cruise Cut Short: A Survey of the Increasing Regulatory Influences Over the Athlete-Agent in the National Football League," *Entertainment and Sports Law Journal* 1 (1984): 53; Len Elmore, "The Agent's Role in Professional Sports: An Athlete's Perspective," *Boston Bar Journal* 31 (1987): 613; G. Uberstine and Grad, "Enforceability of Sports Contracts: A Practitioner's Playbook," *Loyola Entertainment Law Journal* 7 (1987): 1; Fox, "Regulating the Professional Sports Agent: Is California in the Right Ball Park?," *Pacific Law Journal* 15 (1984): 1231; Kohn, "Sports Agents Representing Professional Athletes: Being Certified Means Never Having to Say You're Qualified," *Entertainment and Sports Lawyer* 6, no. 3 (winter 1988): 1; Lefferts, "The NFL Players Association's Agent Certification Plan: Is It Exempt from Antitrust Review?," *Arizona Law Review* 26 (1984): 699; Remick and Eisen, "The Personal Manager in the Entertainment and Sports Industries," *Entertainment and Sports Law Journal* 3 (1986): 57; Ring, "An Analysis of Athlete Agent Certification and Regulation: New Incentives with Old Problems," *Loyola Entertainment Law Journal* 7 (1987): 321; Roberts, "Protecting the College Athlete from Unscrupulous Agents," *Sports Lawyer* 5 (fall 1987): 8; Lionel Sobel, "The Regulation of Sports Agents: An Analytical Primer," *Baylor Law Review* 39 (1987): 701; Sullivan, "Remedying Athlete-Agent Abuse: A Securities Law Approach," *Entertainment and Sports Law Journal* 2 (1984): 53; Winter, "Is the Sports Lawyer Getting Dunked? (Non-Lawyer Agents in Professional Sports)," *A.B.A. Journal* 66 (June 1980): 701; "Regulation of Sports Agents: Since at First It Hasn't Succeeded, Try Federal Legislation," *Sports Inc.,* May 30, 1988, p. 42. See also John Weistart and C. Lowell, *The Law of Sports* (Charlottesville, Va.: Michie, 1979), sec. 3.17.

16. See e.g., Bulkeley, "Sports Agents Help Athletes Win—and Keep—Those Super Salaries," *Wall Street Journal,* March 25, 1985, p. 31, sec. 2 col. 4; House Select Committee on Professional Sports, *Inquiry into Professional Sports,* p. 71.

17. David Ware, speech to the National Football League Players Association agent certification meeting, Washington, D.C., April 19, 1989.

18. David Falk, speech at the Seton Hall Sports Law Symposium, Newark, New Jersey, April 28, 1989.

19. Wilkes, interview.

20. Interview with Edward V. King, Jr., Sept. 3, 1989.

21. Ruxin, *Athlete's Guide*, p. 34.

22. Interview with Dr. Michael Jackson, Sept. 11, 1989.

23. Bucky Woy, *Sign 'em Up Bucky: The Adventures of a Sports Agent* (New York: Hawthorn, 1975), p. 46.

24. Bob Woolf, *Behind Closed Doors* (New York: New American Library, 1976), p. 300.

25. Edward V. King, Jr., "Agents: Do They Help or Hurt the Athlete?: Dependency Leads to Abuse," *New York Times*, March 5, 1989, S-9, col. 2.

26. Interview with Philip Closius, Sept. 5, 1989.

27. Agents generally charge athletes on a percentage basis. The rate varies, but for contract negotiations it is generally less than 5 percent. See also G. Schubert, R. K. Smith, and J. Trentadue, *Sports Law* (St. Paul, Minn.: West, 1986), p. 30, which notes that flat-rate fees or some combination may be used. In 1988 the average salary in the National Basketball Association (NBA) was $515,000, in major league baseball (MLB) $424,896, and in the National Football League (NFL) $209,090. See "Congress Moving Up," *USA Today*, Jan. 16, 1989, 6-A, col. 1.

28. National Collegiate Athletic Association, *A Career in Professional Sports: Guidelines That Make Dollars and Sense* (Mission, Kan.: NCAA, 1984), p. 6, quoting Rozier (hereafter cited as *Guidelines*).

29. Powers, "Coaches, Athletes Are Artful Hustlers, Too," *Sporting News*, Nov. 16, 1987, p. 12.

30. Lawrence Taylor and D. Falkner, *L.T. Living on the Edge* (New York: Warner, 1987), p. 74.

31. Bruce Selcraig, "The Deal Went Sour," *Sports Illustrated*, Sept. 15, 1988, p. 32.

32. "Bannon, Ex-Agent: 'No Clean Programs,'" *USA Today*, Dec. 17, 1987, C-1, col. 4.

33. *Guidelines*, p. 4.

34. Craig Neff, "Agents of Turmoil," *Sports Illustrated*, Aug. 3, 1987, p. 36.

35. Craig Neff, "In Hot and Heavy Pursuit," *Sports Illustrated*, Oct. 19, 1987, pp. 84, 85.

36. "Agent: Players' Contracts Had Bonuses of $75 to $100," *USA Today*, Dec. 16, 1987, 9-C, col. 2.

37. *Ibid.*

38. *Bloom v. Harmon*, No. 11059-014 (1987) (Culver, Arb.) at 2.

39. *Ibid.*, p. 5.

40. See "Sports Agent Case Puts Iowa on Trial, Too," *Chicago Tribune*, March 8, 1989, sec. 4, p. 9, col. 1.

41. Brian Bosworth with R. Reilly, *The Boz: Confessions of a Modern Anti-hero* (New York: Charter, 1989), p. 229.

42. See Robbins and Topol, "Influence on the Bench," *Newsday*, April 3, 1988, p. 5.

43. *Ibid.*

44. John Gorman, "'Agent Threatened Me': Bears' Douglass," *Chicago Tribune*, March 16, 1989, sec. 4, p. 1, col. 3.

45. *Ibid.*

46. *Ibid.*

47. See Ruxin, *Athlete's Guide,* pp. 35–40, which outlines the procedure used by UCLA athletes.

48. O'Connell and Welling, "How Leigh Steinberg Rises Above His 'Sleazoid Profession,'" *Business Week,* Jan. 14, 1985, p. 62.

49. Ware, speech.

50. John Culver, speech to the Sports Lawyers Association.

51. Bob Woolf, "Agents on Campus," in R. Lapchick and J. Slaughter, eds., *The Rules of the Game: Ethics in College Sport* (New York: Macmillan for the American Council of Education, 1989), p. 108.

52. R. Berry, W. Gould, and P. Stadohar, *Labor Relations in Professional Sports* (Dover, Mass.: Auburn House, 1986), p. 10, and M. Pachter, *Champions of American Sport* (New York: Abrams, 1981), pp. 265–266.

53. Berry et al., *Labor Relations.*

54. *Ibid.* There were also reports that tennis great Bill Tilden signed with Pyle, which Tilden denied ("Davis Cup Men Deny Signing with Pyle," *New York Times,* Aug. 28, 1926, p. 8), indicating that even in the beginning there were some negative connotations to being associated with an agent.

55. Schulman, "Life of the Touring Pro," *New York Times,* Sept. 11, 1989, C-2, col. 3.

56. Craig Neff, "Den of Vipers," *Sports Illustrated,* Oct. 19, 1987, p. 77.

57. See "Double Play," *Time,* March 21, 1966, p. 94; Mann, "The $1,000,000 Holdout," *Sports Illustrated,* April 14, 1966, p. 26. See also "All-Star Agent Is a High Scorer," *Business Week,* Sept. 20, 1969, p. 153, and "Playing the Money Game," *Time,* March 21, 1969, p. 94.

58. "Playing the Money Game," p. 94.

59. Mann, "$1,000,000 Holdout," pp. 26, 28.

60. "Playing the Money Game," p. 94.

61. Schubert, Smith, and Trentadue, *Sports Law,* pp. 123–127.

62. Roger Noll, "Economics of Sports Leagues," in G. Uberstine, ed., *Law of Professional and Amateur Sports,* sec. 17.03[4] (New York: Clark Boardman Company Ltd., 1988), pp. 17–23.

63. *Ibid.*

64. Roger Kahn, Introduction to Woolf, *Behind Closed Doors,* pp. vii–xiii.

65. *Ibid.*

66. Mike Trope with S. Delsohn, *Necessary Roughness* (Chicago: Contemporary Books, 1987).

67. Johnson and Reid, "Some Offers They Couldn't Refuse," *Sports Illustrated,* May 21, 1979, p. 28.

68. O'Connell and Welling, "How Steinberg Rises Above," p. 62.

69. Mark McCormack, *What They Don't Teach You at Harvard Business School* (New York: Bantam, 1984), and Donald Dell, *Minding Other People's Business* (New York: Villard, 1989).

70. "King Forges NBA Link," *USA Today,* January 16, 1990, sec. 3-C, col. 3.

Chapter 2

1. *Fla. Stat.* §468.451 (West Supp. 1990). See Rodgers, "States Revamp Defense Against Agents," *Sports Lawyer* 6 (winter 1988–1989): 4, n. 1, which cites as states with legislation pending Arizona, Massachusetts, Michigan, Nebraska, New Hampshire, New York, Pennsylvania, South Carolina, Vermont,

and Washington. As will be discussed, the statutes are all fairly similar and incorporate long-standing beliefs regarding the amateur athlete.

2. See Chapter 4.

3. Craig Neff, "Den of Vipers," *Sports Illustrated*, Oct. 19, 1987, p. 76.

4. Powers, "Time to Revise the Game," *Sporting News*, Nov. 16, 1987, p. 10.

5. Goodwin and Goldaper, "Enmeshed in a Tangled Web," *New York Times*, March 15, 1987, sec. 5, p. 1, col. 2; Papanek, "A Lot of Hurt," *Sports Illustrated*, Oct. 19, 1987, p. 89.

6. Speech by Tom Collins to the Sports Lawyers Asociation, May 5, 1990, Santa Monica, California.

7. See Nack, "Thrown for Heavy Losses," *Sports Illustrated*, March 24, 1986, pp. 40, 41.

8. *Ibid.*

9. "Rodri Faces Lawsuits as Investments Fail," *Sports Industry News*, May 22, 1987, p. 182.

10. "Kelly Is Suing His Former Agents," *New York Times*, April 27, 1989, D-30, col. 1.

11. Montgomery, "The Spectacular Rise and Ignoble Fall of Richard Sorkin, Pros' Agent," *New York Times*, Oct. 9, 1977, sec. 5, p. 7, col. 1.

12. *Ibid.*

13. *Ibid.*, p. 15.

14. Fiffer, "Money Misspent, Witness Says," *New York Times*, March 24, 1989, B-11, col. 5.

15. *Ibid.*

16. Liebner, "And One Who Prospered," *Sports Illustrated*, Oct. 19, 1987, p. 96; Gottschalk, "Orel Hershiser Sees a Lot of Pitches Related to Money," *Wall Street Journal*, March 15, 1989, p. 1, col. 4. See also, Yagoda, "What's the Big Deal?," *Philly Sport*, July 1989, p. 30 (discussing successful financial planning by agent Arthur Rosenberg).

17. *Brown v. Woolf*, 554 F. Supp. 1206 (S.D. Ind. 1983).

18. *Ibid.*, p. 1207.

19. Craig Neff, "Den of Vipers," p. 84.

20. "Reggie White's $1.5 Million Suit," *Sports Industry News*, July 28, 1989, p. 229. The suit served as leverage in White's bid for a contract renegotiation.

21. *Detroit Lions, Inc. v. Argovitz*, 580 F. Supp. 542 (E.D. Mich. 1984).

22. *Ibid.*, p. 546.

23. *Ibid.*, p. 547.

24. "Matchpoint: Agents, Antitrust and Tennis," *University of Detroit Law Review* 64 (1987): 481.

25. For an exposé of problems in tennis generally, see M. Mewshaw, *Short Circuit* (New York: Penguin, 1984).

26. Macnow, "Chief of NHL Union Is on Thin Ice," *Philadelphia Inquirer*, July 16, 1989, D-1, col. 1.

27. John Weistart, quoted in Krupa, "Anticipating the Walter Effects," *Sports Inc.*, Aug. 29, 1988, p. 49.

28. "Commission's Study of Student-Athletes Released," *NCAA News*, Dec. 5, 1988, p. 1.

29. See Chapter 5.

30. Cataldi, "In the World of Sports Agents, It's Business as Usual," *Philadelphia Inquirer*, June 13, 1988, C-4, col. 1.

31. An "opportunistic" act is not inappropriately used in economic terms to

mean "self interest seeking with guile" (Oliver Williamson, *Markets and Hierarchies*, p. 26).
32. See Chapter 5.
33. Mike Sullivan, quoted in Cataldi, "In the World of Sports Agents," C-4.

Chapter 3

1. J. Falla, *NCAA: The Voice of College Sports* (Mission, Kan.: NCAA, 1981), p. 13.
2. Richard D. Schultz, speech to Sports Lawyers Association, Washington, D.C., May 12, 1989.
3. Mike Sullivan and Craig Neff, "Shame on You, SMU," *Sports Illustrated*, March 19, 1987, p. 18.
4. $1.8 Million in Losses Faced By Kentucky Under Probation," *Sports Industry News*, May 26, 1989, p. 157.
5. Schultz, speech.
6. NCAA, "Memorandum to Individuals Acting in the Capacity of Player Agents," Sept. 2, 1988 (hereafter cited as NCAA memorandum).
7. Mike Trope with S. Delsohn, *Necessary Roughness* (Chicago: Contemporary Books, 1987), p. 68.
8. Bruce Selcraig, "Agents of Violence," *Sports Illustrated*, April 6, 1987, p. 25.
9. Brown, "Jury Selection Begins in Agents' Trial," *USA Today*, March 1, 1989, C-1, col. 2.
10. Schultz, speech.
11. 29 U.S.C. §141 *et seq.* (1982). For discussion of the applicability of the NLRA to sports see R. Berry, W. Gould, and P. Stadohar, *Labor Relations in Professional Sports* (Dover, Mass.: Auburn House, 1986), pp. 31–34.
12. "NFLPA Regulations Governing Contract Advisors" (hereafter cited as NFLPA Regulations); "MLBPA Regulations Governing Player Agents" (hereafter MLBPA Regulations); and "National Basketball Players Association Regulations Governing Player Agents" (hereafter NBPA Regulations).
13. MLBPA Regulations, p. 3.
14. "Agent Has His Certification Suspended by NBA Union," *Philadelphia Inquirer*, May 31, 1988, E-5, col. 4.
15. See Macnow, "Becoming an Agent," *Philadelphia Inquirer*, Aug. 23, 1987, A-12, col. 2.
16. Robert Ruxin, *An Athlete's Guide to Agents* (Lexington, Mass.: Stephen Greene, 1989), p. 86.
17. Lionel Sobel, "The Regulation of Sports Agents: An Analytical Primer," *Baylor Law Review* 39 (1987): 727. The agreement is enforced with teams in collective bargaining agreements.
18. MLBPA Regulations, p. 2, citing 29 U.S.C. §141 *et seq.* (1982).
19. *Ibid.*, p. 2, citing MLB Collective Bargaining Agreement, art. II.
20. *Ibid.*, p. 2, citing MLB Collective Bargaining Agreement, art. IV. One agent publicly decertified under the program was Jerry Kapstein, not for any improprieties but because he took a management position within the San Diego Padres organization. "Kapstein Decertified," *New York Times*, Nov. 3, 1989, A-28, col. 2.
21. Gene Orza, speech to Sports Lawyers Association, Washington, D.C., May 12, 1989.

22. Sobel, "Regulation of Sports Agents," 732.
23. Doug Allen, memorandum to NFLPA contract advisers, Nov. 1988.
24. Sobel, "Regulation of Sports Agents," p. 735.
25. Orza, speech.
26. There is a degree of dissent even among the ranks of agents, with one agent calling for the formation of a new trade association. See Rosenblatt, "Agent Interests: Can ARPA Do the Job?," *Sports Inc.*, Nov. 16, 1987, p. 98.
27. American Bar Association (ABA), Model Code of Professional Responsibility (1970); ABA, Model Rules of Professional Conduct (1983).
28. G. Schubert, R. K. Smith, and J. Trentadue, *Sports Law* (St. Paul, Minn.: West, 1986), pp. 144–145.
29. *Shapero v. Kentucky Bar Associations*, 108 S. Ct. 1916, 100 L. Ed. 2d 475 (1988) (ruling that attorneys may solicit clients via direct mail).

Chapter 4

1. *Ala. Code* §§8-26-1–41 (Supp. 1988); *Ark. Legis. Serv.* 544 (1989 Ark. Act 544; 1989 Ark. H.B. 563); *Cal. Lab. Code* §§1500–1547 (West Supp. 1989); *Fla. Stat.* §§468.451–.457 (West Supp. 1990); *Ga. Code Ann.* §§43- 4A-1–18 (Supp. 1988, 1989); *Ind. Code Ann.* §§35-46-4-1–4 (West Supp. 1989); *Iowa Code Ann.* §§9A.1–.12 (West 1989), 722.11 (West Supp. 1989); *Ky. Rev. Stat. Ann.* §§518.010–080 (Supp. 1988); *La. Rev. Stat. Ann.* §§4:421–430 (West 1987, Supp. 1990); *Md. Ann. Code* art. 56, §§632–640 (Supp. 1989); *Mich. Comp. Laws Ann.* §750.411e (West Supp. 1989); *Minn. Stat. Ann.* §325E.33 (West Supp. 1990); *Miss. Code Ann.* §§73-41-1–23 (Supp. 1988); *Nev. Legis. Serv.* 382 (1989 Nev. Ch. 382; 1989 Nev. A.B. 563); *N.C. Gen. Stat.* §§78C-1–62 (West 1988); *Ohio Rev. Code Ann.* §§4771.01–.99 (Supp. 1989); *Okla. Stat. Ann.* tit. 70, §§821.61–.71 (West 1986); *Pa. Stat. Ann.* tit. 18, §7107 (West Supp. 1989): *Tenn. Code Ann.* §§49-7-2101–2109 (Supp. 1989); *Tex. Rev. Civ. Stat. Ann.* art. 8871 (West Supp. 1990).
2. See, e.g., *Fla. Stat.* §468.451.
3. *Ala. Code* §§8-26-4, 8-26-5; *Cal. Lab. Code* §1511; *Fla. Stat.* §468.453; *Ga. Code Ann.* §§43-4A-4, 43-4A-5; *Iowa Code Ann.* §9A.3; *La. Rev. Stat. Ann.* §4:422(c); *Md. Ann. Code* art. 56 §633; *Miss. Code Ann.* §73-41-5; *N.C. Gen. Stat.* §§78C-16, 78C-17; *Okla. Stat. Ann.* tit. 70, §821.62(c); *Tex. Rev. Civ. Stat. Ann.* art. 8871, §2.
4. *Ala. Code* §8-26-14; *Cal. Lab. Code* §1519; *Ga. Code Ann.* §43-4A-13; *Iowa Code Ann.* §9A.6; *Miss. Code Ann.* §73-41-9; *N.C. Gen. Stat.* §78C-17(e); *Okla. Stat. Ann.* tit. 70, §821.62(g); *Tex. Rev. Civ. Stat. Ann.* art. 8871, §2(h).
5. *Ga. Code Ann.* §43-4A-13.
6. *Ky. Rev. Stat. Ann.* §518.010(9); *Mich. Comp. Laws Ann.* §750.411e(3)(g); *Minn. Stat. Ann.* §325E.33(b).
7. *Ala. Code* 8-26-2(2); *Cal. Lab. Code* §1500(b); *La. Rev. Stat. Ann.* §421(A)(4), (5); *N.C. Gen. Stat.* §78C-60; *Okla. Stat. Ann.* tit. 70, 821.61(A)(4), (5).
8. *Ga. Code Ann.* §43-4A-2(2); *Tex. Rev. Civ. Stat. Ann.* art. 8871, §1(a)(5). See also *Md. Ann. Code* art. 56, §632 (2)(i).
9. See Edward V. King, Jr., "Dependency Leads to Abuse," *New York Times*, March 5, 1989, §8-9, col. 2.
10. See Robert Ruxin, *An Athlete's Guide to Agents* (Lexington, Mass.: Stephen Greene, 1989), p. 88, Ruxin notes that only thirty-five agents had registered in

California and none had been fined or jailed. This should be contrasted with a *New York Times* report that eighty sports agents have registered in Alabama since its statute went into effect in 1988. "State May Prosecute," *New York Times,* April 10, 1990, B-10, col. 4.

11. *Cal. Lab Code* §1500(b); *La. Rev. Stat.* Ann. §430; *Miss. Code Ann.* §73-41-21; *N.C. Gen. Stat.* §78C-2(1)(c); *Okla. Stat. Ann.* tit. 70, §821.71.

12. "Texas Fines Former Heisman Winner Firm Under Agent Law," *NCAA News,* Dec. 27, 1989, p. 3.

13. *Ibid.*

14. John Culver, speech to Sports Lawyers Association, Washington, D.C., May 12, 1989.

15. *Iowa Code Ann.* §9A.3(2). See also *N.C. Gen. Stat.* §78C-46 (every sports agent must file irrevocable consent appointing the secretary to receive service of process on his or her behalf).

16. The National Association of Intercollegiate Athletics (NAIA), organized in 1940, has rules similar to those of the NCAA. Its 500 member institutions are generally smaller schools. See *Williams v. Hamilton,* 497 F. Supp. 641 (D.N.H. 1980).

17. *Miss. Code Ann.* §74-41-7(1)(c); *Tenn. Code Ann.* §49-7-2102; *Tex. Civ. Prac. & Rem. Code Ann.* §131.002 (West Supp. 1990).

18. "Former Agent Convicted," *New York Times,* March 2, 1978, B-87, col. 6; *Abernethy v. State,* 545 So. 2d 185 (Ala. Crim. App. 1988).

19. Culver, speech.

20. 18 U.S.C. 1961 *et seq.* (1988).

21. John Gorman, "Lawyers Testify They Gave Lawyers Wrong Information," *Chicago Tribune,* March 30, 1989, sec. 4, p. 2, col. 5.

22. Ruxin, *Athlete's Guide,* p. 90.

23. See, e.g., *Brown v. Woolf,* 554 F. Supp. 1206 (S.D. Ind. 1983); *Burrow v. Probus Management, Inc.,* Civil No. 16840 (N.D. Ga. Aug. 9, 1973) (unpub. order); *Detroit Lions Football Club v. Argovitz,* 580 F. Supp. 542 (E.D. Mich. 1984); *Zinn v. Parrish,* 644 F.2d 360 (4th Cir. 1981).

24. See John Weistart and C. Lowell, *The Law of Sports* (Charlottesville, Va.: Michie, 1979), §3.18, pp. 323–326.

25. Interview with Edward V. King, Jr., Sept. 3, 1989.

26. Interview with Reginald L. Turner, Nov. 8, 1988.

27. Warren A. Seavey, *Handbook of the Law of Agency* (St. Paul, Minn.: West, 1964), §3, p. 3.

28. Johnson and Reid, "Some Offers They Couldn't Refuse," *Sports Illustrated,* May 21, 1979, p. 29.

29. *Ibid.,* p. 35.

30. *Walters v. Fullwood,* 675 F. Supp. 155 (S.D.N.Y. 1987).

31. *Ibid.,* p. 156.

32. *Ibid.,* p. 160

33. *Zinn v. Parrish,* 644 F.2d 360.

34. *Roundball Enterprises v. Richardson,* 616 F. Supp. 1537 (D.C.N.Y. 1985).

35. *Ibid.,* p. 1538.

36. See generally W. Prosser, *The Law of Torts* (5th. ed.) (St. Paul, Minn.: West, 1964), §129.

37. "Double-Agent Suit Filed," *Sports Inc.,* April 25, 1988, p. 3.

38. See, e.g., *Taylor v. Wake Forest University,* 191 S.E.2d 379 (N.C. Ct. App. 1972) cert. den. 192 S.E. 2d 197; *Begley v. Corporation of Mercer University,* 367 F.

Supp. 908 (1973); "Educating Misguided Student Athletes: An Application of Contract Theory, *Columbia Law Review* 85 (1985): 96. See also Woods and Mills, "Tortious Interference with an Athletic Scholarship: A University's Remedy for the Unscrupulous Sports Agent," *Alabama Law Review* 40 (1988): 141.

39. "Alabama to Forfeit $250,000 to N.C.A.A.," *New York Times*, Dec. 16, 1987, B-11, col. 5.

40. Woods and Mills, "Tortious Interference," p. 141.

Chapter 5

1. David C. Young, *The Olympic Myth of Greek Amateur Athletics* (Chicago: Ares, 1985), p. 7.

2. J. Weistart and C. Lowell, *The Law of Sports* (Charlottesville, Va.: Michie, 1979), p. 7, sec. 1.04.

3. *Ibid.*

4. Howard J. Savage, *American College Athletics* (New York: Carnegie Foundation for the Advancement of Teaching, 1929).

5. *Ibid.*, p. 34.

6. Young, *Olympic Myth*, p. 7.

7. *Ibid.*, p. 1. Young notes later (p. 127) that in a single running event the winner received enough money to buy six or seven slaves, one hundred sheep, or three houses.

8. *Ibid.*, p. 7.

9. E. Glader, *Amateurism and Athletics* (West Point, N.Y.: Leisure Press, 1978), p. 54.

10. Young, *Olympic Myth*, p. 7.

11. *Ibid.*, pp. 119–120.

12. *Ibid.*, p. 8.

13. *Ibid.*, p. 9; Young's emphasis. Young notes (p. 51) that Shorey was paraphrasing yet another inaccurate scholar, Percy Gardner.

14. *Ibid.*, p. 8.

15. *Ibid.*, p. 9, n. 3. Young maintains further that this was not, in fact, the first revival of the Olympics. He writes (p. 31) that as early as 1870 a modern Olympiad took place in Athens and there cash prizes were awarded.

16. *Ibid.*, p. 9.

17. *Ibid.*, p. 10.

18. *Ibid.*, p. 9.

19. *Ibid.*, p. 12.

20. *Ibid.*, pp. 12–13.

21. *Ibid.*, p. 13.

22. *Ibid.*, p. 14.

23. M. Pachter, *Champions of American Sport* (New York: Abrams, 1981), p. 195.

24. *Ibid.*

25. Young, *Olympic Myth*, p. 87, n. 84.

26. *Ibid.*, p. 86, citing Avery Brundage, "Why the Olympic Games?," in United States Olympic Committee, *Report: Games of the XIVth Olympiad, London, England* (New York: 1948), pp. 23ff.

26. Young, *Olympic Myth*, 87, n. 84.

27. Glader, *Amateurism and Athletics*, p. 100.

28. *Ibid.*, p. 100, citing H. Hewitt Griftin, *Athletics* (London: George Bell, 1891), pp. 13–14, and H. F. Wilkinson, *Modern Athletics* (London: Frederick Warne, 1868), p. 16.

29. Young, *Olympic Myth*, p. 19.

30. Glader, *Amateurism and Athletics*, p. 15; R. A. Smith, *Sports and Freedom: The Rise of Big-Time College Athletics* (New York: Oxford University Press, 1988), p. 166.

31. Smith, *Sports and Freedom*, p. 166.

32. Glader, *Amateurism and Athletics*, p. 17.

33. Smith, *Sports and Freedom*, pp. 165–166.

34. Savage, *American College Athletics*, p. 36.

35. Young, *Olympic Myth*, p. 22.

36. Smith, *Sports and Freedom*, 169, citing Alexander Agassiz, "Rowing Fifty Years Ago," *Harvard Graduates Magazine* 15 (March 1907): 458; Charles W. Eliot, "In Praise of Rowing," *Harvard Graduates Magazine* 15 (March 1907): 532; and B. W. Crowninshield, "Boating," in F. O. Vaille and H. A. Clark, *The Harvard Book* (Cambridge, Mass.: Welch, Bigelow, 1875), vol. 2, p. 263.

37. Smith, *Sports and Freedom*, p. 171.

38. *Ibid.*, p. 188.

39. *Ibid.*, p. 173.

40. *Ibid.*

41. *Ibid.*

42. *Ibid.*, p. 174.

43. Savage, *American College Athletics*, p. 42.

44. "Eligibility Rules," NCAA Constitution (1906), art. VII.

45. Paul Lawrence, *Unsportsmanlike Conduct: The National Collegiate Athletic Association and the Business of College Football* (New York: Praeger, 1987), p. 24.

46. *Ibid.*, citing NCAA Proceedings (1922), p. 10.

47. B. Rader, American Sports from the Age of Folk Games to the Age of Spectators (Englewood Cliffs, N.J.: Prentice-Hall, 1983), pp. 268–269.

48. Lawrence, *Unsportsmanlike Conduct*, p. 41.

49. *Ibid.*, p. 43.

50. *Walters and Bloom v. Fullwood and Kickliter*, 675 F. Supp. 155 (S.D.N.Y. 1987).

51. *Ibid.*, p. 163.

52. *Ibid.*, p. 163, citing R. J. Hopper, *The Early Greeks* (London: Weidenfeld and Nicolson, 1976).

53. Allen L. Sack, "College Sport and the Student-Athlete," *Journal of Sport and Social Issues* 11, nos. 1–2 (fall/winter 1987–1988): 31–48.

54. *Ibid.*, p. 32.

55. *Ibid.*, p. 41.

56. *Ibid.*

57. *Ibid.*, p. 42.

58. *Ibid.*, p. 43.

59. *Ibid.*, p. 42.

60. *Ibid.*, p. 45.

61. Allen L. Sack, "The Underground Economy of College Sport," paper presented at the Joint Meetings of the North American Society for the Sociology of Sport and the Philosophic Society for the Study of Sport, Washington, D.C., Nov. 10, 1989.

62. *Ibid.*, pp. 5–6.

63. "Illicit Pay in Wide Use, Study Contends," *New York Times,* Nov. 17, 1989, A-34, col. 5.

64. *Ibid.,* A-36, col. 5.

65. *Ibid.,* A-33, col. 2.

66. Sack, "Underground Economy," Table 7.

67. See, e.g., Brennan, "Pros, Cons of Amateurism," *Washington Post,* Sept. 16, 1988, E-2, col. 1; Denlinger, "These Days, It's Take the Money and Run for the Gold," *Washington Post,* Sept. 16, 1988, E-2, col. 3; Dolson, "Let's Leave the Olympics to the True Amateur," *Philadelphia Inquirer,* Sept. 20, 1988, C-10, col. 1.

68. Dolson, "Let's Leave the Olympics," C-10, col. 1.

69. Alvin Chriss, 1986–1987 *TACTRUST Handbook* (Indianapolis: Athletics Congress), pp. 34–35.

70. "Tighter Controls Urged on 'Amateur' Trust Funds," *Sports Industry News,* April 14, 1989, p. 112. "Amateurs' Use of Money Assailed," *New York Times,* April 12, 1989, A-21, col. 4.

71. "A Farewell to Amateurism," *New York Times,* July 15, 1989, p. 47, col. 1.

72. Joe Paterno with B. Asbell, *Paterno: By the Book* (New York: Random House, 1989), p. 184.

73. *Ibid.*

74. NCAA Bylaw 12.1.2, 1989.

75. NCAA Bylaw 15.2.6, 1989.

76. NCAA Bylaw 15.02.4, 1989.

77. NCAA Bylaw 15.2.6. The NCAA is now discussing allowing student athletes in track and field and gymnastics to earn endorsement and other income. See "NCAA Panel Eyes New Rules for Track, Gymnastics Amateurs," *Sports Industry News,* Oct. 21, 1988, p. 325; Krupa, "NCAA May Ok Endorsements," *Sports Inc.,* Oct. 17, 1988, p. 50.

78. See Black, "A Hard Look at Agents, Part II," *Sport,* Dec. 1979, p. 77.

79. "NCAA Aides Urge New Rules Permitting Agent Contracts," *Sports Industry News,* May 29, 1987, p. 170, quoting NCAA official Doug Johnson.

80. "Palmer Says He Accepted Payments," *Philadelphia Inquirer,* July 23, 1988, D-1, col. 6.

81. *Wall Street Journal,* Sept. 4, 1987, p. 13, col. 1.

82. Rhoden, "Rewards of Final Four: Lots of Pride and Profit," *New York Times,* March 31, 1989, A-18, col. 1.

83. Interview with Philip Closius, Sept. 5, 1989.

84. Gerard, "In $1 Billion Deal, CBS Locks Up N.C.A.A. Basketball Tournament," *New York Times,* Nov. 22, 1989, p. 1, col. 5, D-20, col. 4.

Chapter 6

1. R. A. Smith, *Sports and Freedom: The Rise of Big-Time College Athletics* (New York: Oxford University Press, 1988), p. 147.

2. *Ibid.*

3. *Ibid.*

4. Gup, "Playing to Win in Vegas," *Time,* April 3, 1989, p. 57.

5. Smith, *Sports and Freedom,* p. 148.

6. *Ibid.*

7. J. F. Rooney, *The Recruiting Game* (Lincoln: University of Nebraska Press, 1987), p. xv.

8. *Ibid.*, p. 178.

9. NCAA Bylaw 15.2.4.1.

10. *Ibid.*

11. Roger Noll, "The Economics of Intercollegiate Sports," unpub. paper on file with the author.

12. Gary Becker, "The NCAA: A Cartel in Sheepskin Clothing," *Business Week*, Sept. 14, 1987, p. 24.

13. *Ibid.*

14. Interview with Edward V. King, Jr., Sept. 3, 1989.

15. *Ibid.*

16. Interview with Anita DeFrantz, Oct. 10, 1989.

17. Interview with Reginald Wilkes, Sept. 11, 1989.

18. *Ibid.*

19. *Ibid.*

20. Richard D. Schultz, speech to Sports Lawyers Association, Washington, D.C., May 12, 1989.

21. Agent Bob Woolf suggests that the schools provide this insurance. The buying of a policy to protect the athlete against a career-ending injury is a technique used by some agents to attract clients (Woolf, "Agents on Campus," in R. Lapchick and J. Slaughter, eds., *The Rules of the Game: Ethics in College Sport* [New York: Macmillan for the American Council of Education, 1989], p. 105).

22. "Playing the Money Game," *Time*, March 21, 1969, p. 94.

23. Kevin Mulligan, "La Salle Riding the L-Train," *Philadelphia Daily News*, May 9, 1989, p. 66, col. 1.

24. NCAA Bylaw 12.51.1.

25. See Wieberg, "Getting a Foot in the Door: Shoe Companies Make an Imprint on College Basketball," *USA Today*, Dec. 11, 1986, C-1, col. 3.

26. Interview with Pam Lester, Sept. 6, 1989.

27. Jack Friedenthal, speech to Sports Lawyers Association, Washington, D.C., May 12, 1989.

28. Martz, "Payoffs: The Growing Scandal," *Newsweek*, Feb. 23, 1976, p. 26 at 33.

29. Lawrence, *Unsportsmanlike Conduct*, p. 22.

30. Paul Lawrence, pp. 48–52.

31. *Ibid.*

Chapter 7

1. "Senator Wants Athletes to Stay in School," *NCAA News*, May 3, 1989. For a contrasting viewpoint see Donald Kennedy, "So What If College Players Turn Pro Early?" *New York Times*, Jan. 28, 1990, E-21, col. 2, where the president of Stanford University, Donald Kennedy, makes a strong argument for the NFL to draft underclassmen. He concludes by stating: "Who wouldn't like it? The NCAA and the institutions that are practicing athletic exploitation, poorly disguised as academic compassion. That by itself should tell you it's a pretty good idea."

2. See Forbes, "Juniors to be Permitted in Draft Under Rule Revision," *USA Today*, Feb. 16, 1990, 6-C.

3. See also Shannon, "Agents Should Be Part of a Changing College Scene," *New York Times*, Nov. 30, 1980, §5, p. 2, col. 1.

4. See Eskenazi, "Decision on Draft Raises Questions," *New York Times*, Aug. 23, 1987, 5-8, col. 5; "Heyward to Be in NFL Draft," *New York Times*, April 5, 1988, A-22, col. 4.

5. Eskenazi, "Decision on Draft."

6. See, e.g., Frederick C. Klein, "College Football: Keeping 'em Barefoot," *Wall Street Journal*, Sept. 4, 1987, p. 13, col. 1.

7. Eskenazi, "Decision on Draft," 5-8, col. 5.

8. *Ibid.*

9. *Ibid.* See also Forbes, "College Football's Latest Mess Its Own Fault, Not NFL's," *USA Today*, Aug. 31, 1987, C-6, col. 1.

10. In a U.S. District Court opinion, Robert F. Boris successfully fought to have a United States Football League rule against drafting college athletes before their classes graduate declared illegal. The court found that the rule against drafting underclassmen constituted a group boycott and violated the United States antitrust laws. *Boris v. United States Football League*, U.S. District Court (C.D. Co.) No CV 83-4980 LEW (Kx), Feb. 28, 1984.

11. See *Denver Rockets v. All-Pro Management, Inc.*, 325 F. Supp. 1049 (C.D. Cal. 1971), injunction reinstated *sub nom. Haywood v. Nat'l Basketball Ass'n*, 401 U.S. 1204 (1971). "Herschel Walker v. National Football League: A Hypothetical Lawsuit Challenging the Propriety of the National Football League's Four-or-Five Year Rule Under the Sherman Act," *Pepperdine Law Review* 9 (1982): 603, which maintains that the NFL's rule against drafting [underclassmen] would survive antitrust scrutiny only if it would develop a rule that evaluates the physical capabilities of a student athlete to compete in the NFL (p. 640). See also Burkow and Slaughter, "Should Amateur Athletes Resist the Draft?," *Black Law Journal* 7, no. 2, (Jan. 1981): 314–346.

12. "Herschel Walker v. National Football League," p. 630.

13. *Ibid.*, nn. 159, 160.

14. *Ibid.*

15. Phillips, "How 'bout Them Dawgs," *Time*, Dec. 1, 1980, p. 102 at 103.

16. The physical growth required for professional football is rarely achieved by the athlete prior to the graduation of his class from college. Dr. Donald V. Stevenson, a sports medicine specialist in Los Angeles, confirms a view expressed by Dr. Clarence L. Shields, the Los Angeles Rams team physician, that twenty-two is the rough age of peak athletic ability. He makes a strong qualifying statement concerning the potential effect of a strict training regimen on the peak's being reached earlier or later (telephone interview with Stevenson, Jan. 20, 1989; confirming statement by Shields in "Hershel Walker v. National Football League," p. 630, n. 159).

17. NCAA Professional Sports Liaison Committee, Minutes, Oct. 20, 1988, p. 2.

18. There are examples to the contrary since the NCAA does perceive the dilemma of this eligibility issue.

19. Robert Ruxin, *An Athlete's Guide to Agents* (Lexington, Mass.: Stephen Greene Press, 1989), p. 41.

20. Len Elmore, "The Agent's Role in Professional Sports: An Athlete's Perspective," *Boston Bar Journal* 31 (1987): 6.

21. Clearly the advice of the sports agent in this regard may not be the most

unbiased; the sooner the student athlete becomes a professional the sooner the agent can receive his or her fee.

22. Joe Paterno with B. Asbell, *Paterno: By the Book* (New York: Random House, 1989), p. 185.

23. *Ibid.*

24. Robbins and Topol, "Influence on the Bench," *Newsday*, April 3, 1988, p. 5.

25. NCAA Bylaw 12.3.1.

26. Published by the NCAA and written by Robert H. Ruxin.

27. For example, the NBA already requires attendance at a three-day seminar for rookies to discuss matters such as drugs, investments, and life on the road. See Goldaper, "Strickland Learns from First Mistake," *New York Times*, Oct. 24, 1988, C-2, col. 5.

28. Richard D. Schultz, speech to Sports Lawyers Association, Washington, D.C., May 12, 1989. Robert Ruxin writes that "approximately seventy" Division 1 NCAA schools have panels (Ruxin, *Athlete's Guide*, p. 34).

29. Jack Friedenthal, speech to Sports Lawyers Association, Washington, D.C., May 12, 1989.

30. Interview with Dr. Michael Jackson, Sept. 11, 1989.

31. *Ibid.*

32. *Ibid.*

33. Interview with Reginald Wilkes, Sept. 11, 1989.

34. Ruxin, *Athlete's Guide*, p. 34.

35. Interview with Craig Fenech, Nov. 7, 1989.

36. Albert M. Witte, speech to NCAA Career Counseling Panel, Kansas City, Mo., Dec. 3, 1989.

37. *Ibid.*

38. NCAA Minutes, Oct. 20, 1988, p. 3.

Chapter 8

1. Waugh, "Shake 'em Hard in the Sports Side," *National Law Journal*, April 3, 1989, p. 8.

2. John Culver, speech to Sports Lawyers Association, Washington, D.C., May 12, 1989.

3. Hochberg, "The State of Agent Legislation," *Sports Inc.*, May 30, 1988, p. 43.

4. Kohn, "Sports Agents Representing Professional Athletes: Being Certified Means Never Having to Say You're Qualified," *Entertainment and Sports Lawyer* 6, no. 3 (winter 1988): 17.

5. *City of Oakland v. Oakland Raiders*, 174 Cal. App. 3d 414 (1985). For a thorough discussion of the related preemption and federalism issue as well as the use of the supremacy clause, see Wolfson, "Preemption and Federalism: The Missing Link," *Hastings Constitutional Law Quarterly*, 16 (Fall 1988): 69. See also *Partee v. San Diego Chargers Football Co.*, 34 Cal. App. 3d 378, 194 *Cal. Rptr.* 367, 668 P.2d 674, which reaches a similar decision in holding that the NFL requires nationally uniform regulation and that it would be unnecessarily burdened if state antitrust laws applied.

6. See, e.g., *Ga. Code Ann.* 43-4A-7(a) (e.g., may refuse registration upon proof of false statements in application, prior misappropriation of funds,

embezzlement, theft, or fraud); *Ala. Code* §8-26-7 (same as Georgia); *Tex. Rev. Civ. Stat. Ann.* art. 887 §2; *Okla. Stat. Ann.* tit. 70 §821.62(c)(4); *Miss. Code Ann.* §4(10)(a) and (b) (same as Georgia); *La. Rev. Stat. Ann.* §4:422(c)(3); *Iowa Code Ann.* §9A.3(1)(e) (all felony and misdemeanor convictions) and (f) (all financial interest of partners, associates and profit sharers, excluding bona fide employees).

7. "Walters, Alabama Settle Dispute over Signings," *Sports Industry News,* May 20, 1988, p. 156.

8. Craig Neff, "Soft Time," *Sports Illustrated,* May 23, 1988, p. 13.

9. "Agent Conviction Thrown Out by Alabama Appeals Panel," *Sports Industry News,* Jan. 6, 1989, p. 5. *Abernethy v. State,* 545 So. 2d 185 (Ala. Cr. App. 1988).

10. Waugh, "Shake 'em Hard," p. 8.

11. "Criminal Penalties Imposed in Agent Contract Case," *Sports Industry News,* April 28, 1989, p. 125.

12. Burleigh, "Sports Law and Representation: More Agents Than Players in Lucrative Field?," *Chicago Daily Law Bulletin* 133 (Oct. 7, 1987): 16. See, e.g., R. Berry, W. Gould, and P. Stadohar, *Labor Relations in Professional Sports* (Dover Mass.: Auburn House, 1986), 255–256, which notes that, regarding franchise relocations, "Congress will not at length do nothing and leave the disposition of the antitrust problems to the courts under existing law."

13. Sing, "Despite Reforms, Abuses Still Suspected on Wall St.," *Los Angeles Times,* Dec. 24, 1988, p. 1, col. 3.

14. There are currently more than 140 uniform laws. See Directory of Uniform Acts and Codes, U.L.A. (1989 West Supp).

15. See, e.g., Uniform Arbitration Act, Explanation, 7 U.L.A. IV (1985).

16. The National Conference of Commissioners on Uniform State Laws was organized in 1892. The objective of the conference is to promote uniformity in state law on all subjects where the states agree uniformity is desirable.

17. The majority of states provide the Governor or legislature with express legislative authority to appoint an average of four commissioners for three-year terms.

18. Transcripts of the organization's activities and approved acts are listed in the Annual Proceedings.

19. Therefore, each act incorporates criticisms and recommendations of commissioners, who represent legal expertise from various parts of the country.

20. See James White and Robert Summers, *Uniform Commercial Code* (3d ed.; St. Paul, Minn.: West, 1988), p. 20.

21. Interview with Craig Fenech, Nov. 7, 1989.

22. Interview with Reginald Wilkes, Sept. 11, 1989.

23. "Agent Has His Certification Suspended by NBA Union," *Philadelphia Inquirer,* May 31, 1988, 5-E, col. 4; Comte, "Deals May Be Invalid," *Sports Inc.,* May 16, 1988, p. 3.

24. Comte, "Deals May Be Invalid," p. 3.

25. *Ibid.*

26. Macnow, "Becoming an Agent," *Philadelphia Inquirer,* Aug. 23, 1987, A-12, col. 2.

27. Neff, "Agents of Turmoil," *Sports Illustrated,* Aug. 3, 1987, p. 78.

28. One athlete, when informed that his agent was not certified, noted, "I'm

still not quite clear on why he can't negotiate contracts" (Comte, "Deals May Be Invalid," p. 3).

29. "Fee Dispute Marks Beckman Grievance," *Sports Industry News*, June 2, 1989, p. 168.

Chapter 9

1. G. Miller, *Behind the Olympic Rings* (Lynn, Mass.: H. O. Zimman, 1979), p. 55.

2. *Los Angeles Rams v. Cannon*, 185 F. Supp. 717 (S.D.C.C. 1960).

3. Walter Camp Papers, Box 44, Folder 2, Manuscripts and Archives, Yale University.

4. Data complied by Allen Sack from the *Chronicle of Higher Education*.

5. Roger Noll, "The Economics of Intercollegiate Athletics," unpublished paper in author's files, p. 20.

6. "No More Incentives," *New York Times*, Aug. 16, 1989, D-22, col. 3, which notes that one manager was paying players a dollar for their first hit and five dollars for home runs and another was paying ten cents for each hit, twenty-five cents for an outstanding fielding play, and a dollar per home run.

7. Interview with Edward V. King, Jr., Sept. 3, 1989.

8. Dan Moldea, *Interference: How Organized Crime Influences Professional Football*, (New York: William Morrow, 1989), p. 409.

9. "Valukas Warns Mafia May Invade College Sports, Agents' Ranks," *Sports Industry News*, April 28, 1989, p. 125.

10. Eskanazi, "Two Men Who Aided Shackleford," *New York Times*, March 4, 1990, 8-1, col. 6.

11. Moldea, *Interference*, p. 409.

12. For recent studies on the problems generally, see R. Lapchick and J. Slaughter, eds., *The Rules of the Game: Ethics in College Sports* (New York: Macmillan for the American Council on Education, 1989), and R. Telander, *The Hundred Yard Lie: The Corruption of College Football and What We Can Do to Stop It* (New York: Simon & Schuster, 1989).

13. T. Tinling, *Tinling: Sixty Years in Tennis* (London: Sidgwick & Jackson, 1983), p. 61.

14. Howard J. Savage, *American College Athletics* (New York: Carnegie Foundation for the Advancement of Teaching, 1929), p. vi.

15. Fiffer, "Two Agents Get Prison Terms," *New York Times*, June 20, 1989, B-9, col. 3.

Index

This book was set in Baskerville and Eras typefaces. Baskerville was designed by John Baskerville at his private press in Birmingham, England, in the eighteenth century. The first typeface to depart from oldstyle typeface design, Baskerville has more variation between thick and thin strokes. In an effort to insure that the thick and thin strokes of his typeface reproduced well on paper, John Baskerville developed the first wove paper, the surface of which was much smoother than the laid paper of the time. The development of wove paper was partly responsible for the introduction of typefaces classified as modern, which have even more contrast between thick and thin strokes.

Eras was designed in 1969 by Studio Hollenstein in Paris for the Wagner Typefoundry. A contemporary script-like version of a sans-serif typeface, the letters of Eras have a monotone stroke and are slightly inclined.